Contents

BETTER HOMES AND GARDENS BOOKS

Editorial Director: Don Dooley
Managing Editor: Malcolm E. Robinson   Art Director: John Berg
Production and Copy Chief: Lawrence D. Clayton
Assistant Art Director: Randall Yontz
Food Editor: Nancy Morton
Senior Writer: Sharyl Heiken
Associate Editors: Elizabeth Strait, Sandra Granseth,
Rosemary C. Hutchinson, Diane Nelson
Assistant Editor: Flora Szatkowski
Designers: Candy Carleton, Faith Berven,
Harijs Priekulis, Sheryl Veenschoten

Our seal assures you that every recipe in the *Chicken and Turkey Cook Book* is endorsed by the Better Homes and Gardens Test Kitchen. Each recipe is carefully tested for family appeal, practicality, and deliciousness.

About Poultry

Chicken . . . turkey . . . duck . . . goose . . . quail . . . pheasant . . . Cornish game hen . . . squab . . . partridge—these are just a few of the poultry birds available. And as there are so many birds, so are there innumerable delectable and imaginative ways to prepare them—from stuffing and roasting, braising in wine, simmering in stew, oven frying, and grilling to the avant-garde microwave cooking. This is possible because poultry is so versatile.

Many of the birds are available year-round. Chicken and turkey are both in ready supply throughout the year—chicken marketed fresh, frozen, or canned and turkey most often marketed frozen. Even Cornish game hens (small, specially bred chickens) are found regularly in the store's frozen food department. You may have to look for frozen duckling and goose. Most supermarkets and meat markets do carry them during the holidays and often will special-order them for you. Whichever type of bird you purchase, if it comes from a commercial market, you'll find it completely cleaned and ready to use.

Also, you don't have to stick with whole birds. Look for chicken and turkey in halves or quarters. And if you have a preference for certain pieces, buy just drumsticks, thighs, breasts, or wings. Beyond this, you can choose boneless turkey roasts and pre-cooked rolls, plus self-basting and pre-stuffed turkeys, turkeys with a built-in meat thermometer, and other innovative products. All of these forms adapt to hearty, home-style dishes or glamorous entrées.

Although more difficult to locate than domestic birds, game birds are just as versatile. Wild duck and goose, pheasant, quail, and squab are prized as culinary delicacies. Fortunately, you needn't be a hunter to enjoy them—some domestically raised game birds are marketed frozen.

Most poultry responds favorably to at least eight different cooking methods—roasting, broiling, grilling, frying, stewing, braising, microwave cooking, and crockery cooking. Tender, young birds are suitable for nearly any poultry recipe. Mature birds, however, are best braised or stewed. It's the moist, slow cooking that makes these birds tender. You can tell the difference between young and mature birds by looking at the name on the package. Young chickens may be labeled broiler-fryers or roasters, young turkeys are called young hens or toms, and young ducks are called ducklings. You'll find mature chickens labeled hens or stewing chickens and mature turkeys labeled yearlings.

Having selected the bird and the cooking method, combine them with the many delicious and exciting, top-rated recipes you'll discover on the following pages.

If you can remember feasting on an extra helping of your mother's *Chicken and Dumplings*, this version will bring back some childhood memories (see recipe, page 35). To make this home-cooked favorite, simmer chicken in the flavorful broth, then top with parsley dumplings and steam till light and fluffy.

Family Favorites

Whether you're looking for a platter of crispy fried chicken for Sunday dinner or a meal-in-one casserole after a busy day, in this section, you'll discover home-cooked poultry to fit any family occasion.

Some of these recipes—Chicken and Homemade Noodles, Stewed Chicken—will bring nostalgic aromas to your kitchen. Others, such as Chicken-Noodle Casserole, are exceptional versions of dishes you may already serve. Still others will be tasty new additions to your collection of family recipes.

And, since you'll find many opportunities to use leftovers, you can cater to your family budget as well as your family's appetite.

As a bonus, certain recipes in the book feature microwave- and crockery-cooking directions.

Next time your family gathers for a backyard barbecue, grill *Hickory-Smoked Turkey* (see recipe, page 18) and foil-wrapped potatoes. Cook the potatoes along with the bird, then top with shredded Swiss cheese and sliced green onion just before serving.

Old-Fashioned Fried Chicken

Tender Pan-Fried Chicken

¼ cup all-purpose flour
1½ teaspoons salt
1 teaspoon paprika
¼ teaspoon pepper
1 2½- to 3-pound broiler-fryer
   chicken, cut up
2 tablespoons cooking oil *or*
   shortening

In a paper or plastic bag combine flour, salt, paprika, and pepper. Add 2 or 3 chicken pieces at a time and shake to coat pieces evenly.

In a 12-inch skillet heat oil or shortening. Place meaty chicken pieces toward center and remaining pieces around edge. Brown over medium heat about 15 minutes, turning as necessary to brown evenly. Reduce heat; cover tightly. Cook for 30 minutes. Uncover; cook till tender, 5 to 10 minutes. Serves 4.

Oven-Fried Chicken

¼ cup butter *or* margarine,
   melted
½ teaspoon salt
¼ teaspoon pepper
1 2½- to 3-pound broiler-fryer
   chicken, cut up
1 cup crushed cornflakes *or*
   crushed potato chips *or* ½ cup
   fine dry bread crumbs

Combine butter, salt, and pepper. Brush chicken with butter mixture, then roll in cornflakes, potato chips, *or* bread crumbs. Place chicken, skin side up, without touching in an ungreased, large shallow baking pan. Bake at 375° till tender, about 1 hour. Do not turn. Season to taste with salt. Makes 4 servings.

◀ **A crunchy coating and nutty flavor** characterize these oven-crisped chicken breasts. The peach halves bake with *Bran-Flake Chicken and Peaches* the last few minutes (see recipe, page 10).

Crisp Pan-Fried Chicken

¼ cup all-purpose flour
1½ teaspoons salt
1 teaspoon paprika
¼ teaspoon pepper
1 2½- to 3-pound broiler-fryer
   chicken, cut up
2 tablespoons cooking oil *or*
   shortening

In a paper or plastic bag combine flour, salt, paprika, and pepper. Add 2 or 3 chicken pieces at a time and shake to coat pieces evenly. (If desired, omit coating the chicken with flour mixture; continue as directed.)

In a 12-inch skillet heat cooking oil or shortening. Place meaty chicken pieces toward the center and remaining pieces around the edge. Turn heat to medium-low and cook slowly, *uncovered,* till chicken is tender, 55 to 60 minutes, turning chicken occasionally. Drain on paper toweling. Makes 4 servings.

Pan- and Oven-Fried Chicken

Adapt this easy technique to fry large quantities—

¼ cup all-purpose flour
1½ teaspoons salt
1 teaspoon paprika
¼ teaspoon pepper
    • • •
1 2½- to 3-pound broiler-fryer
   chicken, cut up
2 tablespoons cooking oil *or*
   shortening

In a paper or plastic bag combine flour, salt, paprika, and pepper. Add 2 or 3 chicken pieces at a time and shake to coat evenly.

In a 12-inch oven-going skillet, heat oil. Brown chicken in hot oil over medium heat about 15 minutes, turning to brown evenly.

Transfer skillet to a 375° oven. *Or,* remove chicken from skillet and place, skin side up, in an ungreased, large shallow baking pan. Bake at 375° till chicken is tender, 35 to 45 minutes. Do not turn. Makes 4 servings.

French-Fried Chicken

Simmer one cut-up 2½- to 3-pound broiler-fryer **chicken** in lightly **salted water** for 20 minutes; drain. Combine 1¼ cups all-purpose **flour,** 1 teaspoon **baking powder,** and 1 teaspoon **salt.** Combine 1 beaten **egg,** 1 cup **milk,** and ¼ cup **cooking oil.** Add dry ingredients; beat smooth. Pour **cooking oil** into deep skillet to depth of 1¼ inches; heat to 350°. Regulate heat so chicken fries at 325°. Dip chicken in batter. Fry, a few pieces at a time, in hot oil till golden, about 5 minutes, turning once. Drain well; keep warm while frying remaining chicken. Serves 4.

Southern-Style Fried Chicken

> 2 2½- to 3-pound broiler-fryer
>   chickens, cut up
> 2 cups all-purpose flour
> 2 cups buttermilk
>   Cooking oil

Season chicken with salt and pepper. Coat with some of the flour, then dip in buttermilk; coat again with remaining flour. Pour oil into deep skillet to depth of 1¼ inches; heat to 350°. Regulate heat so chicken fries at 325°. Fry, a few pieces at a time, in hot oil till tender, 12 to 15 minutes; turn once. Drain well. Serve hot or chilled. Makes 8 servings.

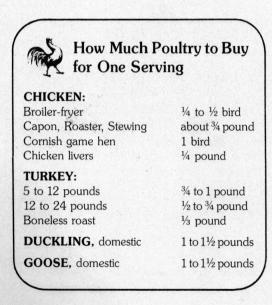

How Much Poultry to Buy for One Serving

CHICKEN:

Broiler-fryer	¼ to ½ bird
Capon, Roaster, Stewing	about ¾ pound
Cornish game hen	1 bird
Chicken livers	¼ pound

TURKEY:

5 to 12 pounds	¾ to 1 pound
12 to 24 pounds	½ to ¾ pound
Boneless roast	⅓ pound
DUCKLING, domestic	1 to 1½ pounds
GOOSE, domestic	1 to 1½ pounds

Maryland Fried Chicken

> 1 slightly beaten egg
> ¼ cup milk
> ⅔ cup finely crushed crackers
> ½ teaspoon salt
> ¼ teaspoon pepper
> 1 2½- to 3-pound broiler-fryer
>   chicken, cut up
> 2 tablespoons shortening
> 1 cup milk
>   Cream Gravy for Fried Chicken
>   (see page 66)

Combine egg and ¼ cup milk. Combine crackers, salt, and pepper. Dip chicken in egg mixture, then roll in crumbs. In skillet brown chicken in hot shortening about 15 minutes, turning to brown evenly. Add 1 cup milk. Reduce heat; cover tightly. Simmer for 35 minutes. Uncover; cook till tender, about 10 minutes. Prepare gravy from pan drippings. Makes 4 servings.

Bran-Flake Chicken and Peaches

Oven-fried chicken pictured on page 8—

> ½ cup slightly crushed bran
>   flakes (¾ cup uncrushed)
> ¼ cup shelled sunflower seed,
>   chopped
> ½ teaspoon seasoned salt
> ¼ cup butter *or* margarine,
>   melted
> 2 tablespoons lemon juice
> ½ teaspoon salt
> 3 whole large chicken breasts,
>   halved lengthwise, *or* 6 whole
>   small chicken breasts
> 1 16-ounce can peach halves,
>   drained

In paper or plastic bag combine bran flakes, sunflower seed, and seasoned salt. Blend melted butter, lemon juice, and salt. Brush chicken breasts with butter mixture, then shake, one at a time, in bran mixture to coat lightly. (Reserve remaining lemon-butter.)

Place chicken, skin side up, in an ungreased, large shallow baking pan. Bake at 375° for 40 minutes. Do not turn. Meanwhile, brush peaches with reserved lemon-butter. Arrange in pan with chicken; continue baking till chicken is tender, 5 to 10 minutes. Makes 6 servings.

Sesame Picnic Chicken

⅔ cup finely crushed saltine
    crackers (20 crackers)
¼ cup sesame seed, toasted
½ teaspoon salt
¼ cup butter *or* margarine
 1 2½- to 3-pound broiler-fryer
    chicken, cut up
¼ cup milk

Combine crackers, sesame seed, and salt. Melt butter in a 13x9x2-inch baking dish. Dip chicken in milk, then roll in crumbs. Dip skin side in butter. Turn; arrange, skin side up, in baking dish. Bake at 375° about 1 hour. Do not turn. Serve hot or chilled. Makes 4 servings.

Oven Parmesan Chicken

¼ cup seasoned fine dry bread
    crumbs
¼ cup grated Parmesan cheese
 2 tablespoons snipped parsley
¼ teaspoon dried oregano, crushed
 1 2½- to 3-pound broiler-fryer
    chicken, cut up
¼ cup butter *or* margarine, melted

Combine crumbs, cheese, parsley, and oregano. Brush chicken with butter, then roll in crumb mixture. Place, skin side up, in ungreased, large shallow baking pan. Sprinkle with any remaining crumb mixture. Bake at 375° till tender, 50 to 60 minutes. Do not turn. Makes 4 servings.

Tater-Coated Chicken

 1 slightly beaten egg
¼ cup grated Parmesan cheese
 2 tablespoons water
½ teaspoon salt
 2 tablespoons butter *or* margarine
 1 2½- to 3-pound broiler-fryer
    chicken, cut up
 1 cup packaged instant mashed
    potato flakes

Combine egg, cheese, water, and salt. Melt butter in large shallow baking pan. Dip chicken in egg mixture; roll in potato flakes. Place in pan, skin side up. Bake at 375° for 50 to 60 minutes. Do not turn. Makes 4 servings.

Curry and Parsley Chicken

½ cup fine dry bread crumbs
¼ cup snipped parsley
 1 tablespoon curry powder
 1 teaspoon onion salt
½ teaspoon salt
⅛ teaspoon ground ginger
 1 slightly beaten egg
 2 tablespoons water
 1 2½- to 3-pound broiler-fryer
    chicken, cut up
¼ cup all-purpose flour
 2 tablespoons cooking oil

In paper or plastic bag combine bread crumbs, parsley, curry powder, onion salt, salt, and ginger. Combine slightly beaten egg and water. Coat chicken pieces with flour, then dip in egg mixture. Shake chicken pieces in crumb mixture, a few at a time, to coat evenly.

In 12-inch skillet brown chicken in hot oil about 15 minutes, turning to brown evenly. Reduce heat; cover tightly. Cook for 30 minutes. Uncover; cook till chicken is tender, 5 to 10 minutes longer. Makes 4 servings.

Orange-Basil Chicken

 1 slightly beaten egg
½ of a 6-ounce can frozen orange
    juice concentrate, thawed
    (⅓ cup)
 2 tablespoons soy sauce
½ cup fine dry bread crumbs
1½ teaspoons dried basil, crushed
 1 teaspoon salt
 1 teaspoon grated orange peel
¼ cup butter *or* margarine
 1 2½- to 3-pound broiler-fryer
    chicken, cut up

Combine egg, orange juice concentrate, and soy sauce. Mix together bread crumbs, basil, salt, and grated orange peel. Melt butter or margarine in a 13x9x2-inch baking pan.

Dip chicken pieces in orange juice mixture, then roll in crumb mixture. Dip skin side of chicken pieces in melted butter. Turn chicken over and arrange, skin side up, in baking pan. Sprinkle with any remaining crumb mixture. Bake at 375° till chicken is tender, 50 to 60 minutes. Do not turn. Makes 4 servings.

Noodle-Coated Chicken

    1 2½- to 3-pound broiler-fryer
        chicken, cut up
    2 tablespoons butter, melted
    2 tablespoons honey
    1 tablespoon lemon juice
    1½ teaspoons soy sauce
    1 cup finely crushed chow mein
        noodles

Sprinkle chicken with salt and pepper. Place, skin side up, in ungreased 13x9x2-inch baking dish. Bake at 375° for 45 minutes.

Meanwhile, combine melted butter, honey, lemon juice, and soy sauce; stir in noodles. Top chicken with butter mixture. Continue baking till chicken is tender, 10 to 15 minutes more. Do not turn. Skim fat from pan juices; serve juices over chicken. Makes 4 servings.

Chicken Paprika

    ¼ cup all-purpose flour
    1 tablespoon paprika
    1 teaspoon salt
    ¼ teaspoon pepper
    1 2½- to 3-pound broiler-fryer
        chicken, cut up
    2 tablespoons cooking oil
    ½ cup chopped onion
        Sour Cream Gravy (see page 67)

In paper or plastic bag combine flour, paprika, salt, and pepper. Add 2 or 3 chicken pieces at a time; shake to coat evenly. In 12-inch skillet brown chicken in hot oil about 15 minutes, turning to brown evenly. Add onion and ¼ cup water. Reduce heat; cover tightly. Simmer till tender, 30 to 40 minutes. Prepare Sour Cream Gravy from pan drippings. Makes 4 servings.

Golden Cornmeal Chicken

Combine ½ cup yellow **cornmeal**, 1 teaspoon **salt**, ⅛ teaspoon **garlic salt**, and dash **cayenne**. Mix 1 slightly beaten **egg** and 2 tablespoons **water**. Dip one cut-up 2½- to 3-pound broiler-fryer **chicken** in egg; coat lightly with cornmeal mixture. Brown in 2 tablespoons **cooking oil**. Reduce heat; cover tightly. Cook 30 minutes. Uncover; cook 5 to 10 minutes more. Serves 4.

Coconut 'n Curry Chicken

    ½ cup coarsely crushed bran
        flakes
    ¼ cup shredded coconut
    1 teaspoon curry powder
    1 teaspoon salt
    2 whole small chicken breasts,
        halved lengthwise, or 2 chicken
        drumsticks with thighs
    2 tablespoons butter, melted

Combine bran flakes, coconut, curry powder, and salt. Brush chicken with melted butter, then roll in bran flake mixture. Place chicken, skin side up, in ungreased shallow baking pan. Bake at 375° till tender, 40 to 45 minutes. Do not turn. Makes 2 servings.

Pepper Chicken

    2 tablespoons butter, melted
    1 tablespoon bottled steak sauce
    1½ teaspoons coarsely ground black
        pepper or 2 teaspoons
        seasoned pepper
    1 teaspoon salt
    1 2½- to 3-pound broiler-fryer
        chicken, cut up

Combine melted butter, steak sauce, pepper, and salt. Brush chicken pieces with butter mixture. Place, skin side up, in ungreased shallow baking pan. Bake at 375° till tender, 50 to 60 minutes. Do not turn. Makes 4 servings.

Chicken in Chips

    ½ of a 5⅓-ounce can evaporated
        milk (⅓ cup)
    1 tablespoon lemon juice
    ¼ teaspoon paprika
        Dash pepper
    4 chicken drumsticks with thighs
    1¼ cups coarsely crushed potato
        chips (4 cups uncrushed)

Combine evaporated milk, lemon juice, paprika, and pepper. Brush chicken pieces with milk mixture, then roll in potato chips. Place chicken, skin side up, in ungreased shallow baking pan. Bake at 375° till tender, 50 to 60 minutes. Do not turn. Makes 4 servings.

Chicken Wings with Potatoes

Chicken and homemade "fries" shown on page 28—

> ½ cup fine dry bread crumbs
> 3 tablespoons grated Parmesan
>   cheese
> 2 tablespoons snipped parsley
> ½ teaspoon salt
>   Dash garlic powder
>   Dash pepper
> 2 pounds chicken wings
> ¼ cup milk
> 4 medium potatoes, peeled and cut
>   in sticks
> 2 tablespoons butter, melted

Combine first 6 ingredients. Dip chicken in milk, then roll in crumb mixture. Place with potatoes in single layer in ungreased 15½x10½x1-inch baking pan. Drizzle butter over potatoes. Sprinkle with salt and pepper. Bake at 375° for 30 to 35 minutes. Do not turn. Makes 4 servings.

Fried Peanut Butter Chicken

Beat together 1 **egg,** ½ cup **peanut butter,** 1 teaspoon **salt,** and ⅛ teaspoon **pepper.** Blend in ⅔ cup **milk.** Coat one cut-up 2½- to 3-pound broiler-fryer **chicken** with ¼ cup all-purpose **flour,** then with milk mixture. Coat with ¾ cup fine dry **bread crumbs.** Place in ungreased, large shallow baking pan. Bake at 375° till tender, 45 to 50 minutes. Do not turn. Serves 4.

Chicken Italiano

> ¼ cup all-purpose flour
> 2 tablespoons softened butter
> ½ envelope Italian *or* onion salad
>   dressing mix (2 teaspoons)
> ½ teaspoon paprika
> 3 tablespoons water
> 1 2½- to 3-pound broiler-fryer
>   chicken, cut up

In a small bowl thoroughly combine flour, softened butter, salad dressing mix, and paprika. Blend in water. Spread butter mixture over chicken pieces. Place chicken, skin side up, in ungreased, large shallow baking pan. Bake at 375° till chicken is tender, 50 to 60 minutes. Do not turn. Makes 4 servings.

Oven-Crisped Citrus Chicken

> 1 teaspoon grated orange peel
>   (set aside)
> ¼ cup orange juice
> 2 tablespoons lime juice
> 1 2½- to 3-pound broiler-fryer
>   chicken, cut up
> ¼ cup all-purpose flour
> 1 teaspoon salt
> ½ teaspoon chili powder
> ¼ cup butter *or* margarine, melted

Combine orange juice and lime juice in a 13x9x2-inch baking dish; add chicken pieces, turning to coat on all sides. Cover and refrigerate about 2 hours, occasionally tilting dish and spooning juice mixture over chicken. Drain, reserving juices.

In paper or plastic bag combine flour, salt, chili powder, and orange peel. Brush chicken pieces with melted butter, then shake, a few at a time, in flour mixture to coat evenly. Return chicken to baking dish; spoon reserved juices over. Bake at 375° till tender, 50 to 60 minutes. Do not turn. Makes 4 servings.

Barbecue Fried Chicken

> 1 2½- to 3-pound broiler-fryer
>   chicken, cut up
> ¼ cup all-purpose flour
> 1 teaspoon salt
> 2 tablespoons cooking oil
> 1 cup catsup
> ½ cup chopped onion
> ½ cup water
> 1 small clove garlic, minced
> 1 teaspoon salt
> ¼ teaspoon pepper
> 3 tablespoons lemon juice

Coat chicken pieces with a mixture of the flour and the 1 teaspoon salt. In a 12-inch skillet brown chicken in hot oil over medium heat about 15 minutes, turning to brown evenly.

Meanwhile, in a saucepan combine catsup, onion, water, garlic, 1 teaspoon salt, and pepper. Bring to boiling. Simmer, uncovered, for 20 minutes. Remove from heat; blend in lemon juice. Add catsup mixture to chicken. Cover; cook over low heat till tender, 35 to 40 minutes; turn occasionally. Makes 4 servings.

How to Cut Up Chicken

Break bones at hip joints. Cut skin between thighs and body. Grasping a leg in each hand, lift chicken and bend back legs till bones break.

Remove leg and thigh piece from body. Cut between joints as close as possible to the backbone. Repeat on the opposite side.

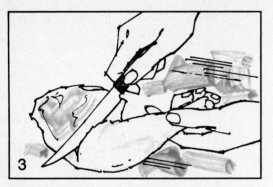

Separate thighs and legs. Locate the knee joint by bending thigh and leg together. Cut through the knee joint of each leg.

Remove wing from body. Start cutting on the inside of wing just over the joint. Cut down through the joint. Remove the other wing.

Divide the body. Place bird on neck end and cut along the breast end of the ribs to the neck. Separate the breast and back section, cutting through the joints. Bend back-piece in half to break at joint; cut through the back-piece at broken joint.

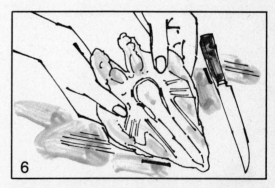

Bone the breast. Cut through white cartilage at V of neck. Using both hands, grasp the small bones on either side. Bend each side back, pushing up with fingers to snap out breastbone.

To split breast: Cut breast in two lengthwise pieces just below the breastbone.

Chicken and Ham Croquettes

2 beaten eggs
2 tablespoons butter *or*
    margarine, melted
¾ cup soft bread crumbs (1 slice)
½ teaspoon dry mustard
    Dash ground nutmeg
    Dash pepper
3 cups ground cooked chicken *or*
    turkey
1 cup ground fully cooked ham
1 beaten egg
½ cup fine dry bread crumbs
    Fat for frying
    Caper Sauce

In mixing bowl combine the 2 beaten eggs, butter, soft bread crumbs, mustard, nutmeg, and pepper. Add chicken and ham; mix well. Chill.

Shape cold chicken mixture into 12 logs, using about ¼ cup mixture for each. Dip logs in the remaining beaten egg, then roll in fine dry bread crumbs. Fry in deep hot fat (365°) for 2½ to 3 minutes. Drain well. Serve with Caper Sauce. Makes 6 servings.

Caper Sauce: In small saucepan melt 2 tablespoons **butter** *or* **margarine;** blend in 2 tablespoons all-purpose **flour.** Stir in ½ cup **milk** and ½ cup **chicken broth;** cook and stir till bubbly. Stir in 1 tablespoon **capers.**

Oven-Easy Chicken Croquettes

2 tablespoons butter *or* margarine
3 tablespoons all-purpose flour
½ cup milk
½ cup chicken broth
2 cups ground *or* finely chopped
    cooked chicken *or* turkey
1 tablespoon snipped parsley
¼ teaspoon salt
⅛ teaspoon dried rosemary,
    crushed
8 slices white bread
1 beaten egg
2 tablespoons butter, melted
    Cranberry-Claret Sauce

Melt the 2 tablespoons butter; blend in flour. Add milk and broth; cook and stir till bubbly. Cool slightly. Add chicken, parsley, salt, and rosemary. Cover; chill several hours.

Trim crusts from bread; cut bread in ½-inch cubes. Shape chicken mixture into 8 balls, using ¼ cup mixture for each. Dip balls in egg, then coat with bread cubes. Place in greased shallow baking pan. Brush with 2 tablespoons melted butter. Bake at 375° till hot and toasted, about 30 minutes. Serve with sauce. Makes 4 servings.

Cranberry-Claret Sauce: Heat together one 8-ounce can jellied **cranberry sauce** and ¼ cup **claret.** Beat till mixture is smooth.

Coating Methods

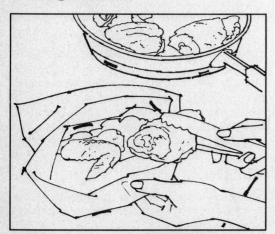

A quick way to coat chicken is to shake the pieces with dry ingredients in a plastic bag. Shake a few at a time till coated evenly.

For another coating method, brush chicken pieces with melted butter or dip in an egg-water mixture, then roll in a crumb mixture.

Poultry—Barbecued and Broiled

Cinnamon-Glazed Chicken

In small saucepan cook ¼ cup chopped **onion** in ¼ cup **butter** *or* **margarine** till tender but not brown. Blend in 1 teaspoon ground **cinnamon** and ½ teaspoon **curry powder;** set aside.

Season one quartered 2½- to 3-pound broiler-fryer **chicken** with **salt**. Place, bone side down, over *medium-hot* coals. Brush with cinnamon mixture. Grill 25 minutes. Turn skin side down; grill 20 minutes more. Stir 2 tablespoons **honey** into cinnamon mixture; brush over chicken. Continue grilling till chicken is tender, 10 to 15 minutes, turning frequently and basting with sauce. Makes 4 servings.

Barbecued Spicy Chicken

    ¼ cup finely chopped onion
    1 clove garlic, minced
    2 tablespoons cooking oil
    ¾ cup catsup
    ⅓ cup vinegar
    1 teaspoon grated lemon peel
    1 tablespoon lemon juice
    1 tablespoon Worcestershire
        sauce
    2 teaspoons sugar
    1 teaspoon dry mustard
    ½ teaspoon salt
    ¼ teaspoon pepper
    ¼ teaspoon bottled hot
        pepper sauce
        • • •
    2 2½- to 3-pound broiler-fryer
        chickens, quartered

Cook onion and garlic in oil till tender but not brown. Stir in remaining ingredients *except* chicken. Simmer, covered, about ½ hour; stir occasionally. Season chicken with salt and pepper. Place, bone side down, over *medium-hot* coals. Grill 25 minutes. Turn skin side down; grill 20 minutes more. Brush barbecue sauce over chicken. Continue grilling till tender, 10 to 15 minutes, turning frequently and basting with sauce. Makes 8 servings.

Grilled Lemon Chicken

Season one quartered 2½- to 3-pound broiler-fryer **chicken** with **salt** and **pepper**. Place chicken pieces, bone side down, over *medium-hot* coals. Grill 25 minutes. Turn skin side down and grill 20 minutes more. Meanwhile, combine ¼ cup light **corn syrup,** 1 teaspoon finely shredded **lemon peel,** 2 tablespoons **lemon juice,** and 1 tablespoon **cooking oil.** Brush both sides of chicken with glaze. Grill till tender, 10 to 15 minutes longer, turning and brushing with glaze occasionally. Makes 4 servings.

Fruit-Turkey Kabobs

    ¾ pound cooked boneless turkey
        roast, cut in twelve 1-inch
        cubes
    1 orange, cut in wedges
    1 firm pear, cut in wedges
    1 green pepper, cut in squares
    4 small spiced crab apples
    ½ cup jellied cranberry sauce
    ½ cup apricot preserves
    ½ cup light corn syrup
    ¼ cup lemon juice
    2 tablespoons butter *or* margarine
    ¼ teaspoon ground cinnamon
        Dash ground cloves

Thread pieces of turkey, orange, pear, green pepper, and a crab apple onto four 10-inch skewers. In saucepan combine remaining ingredients; bring to boiling, stirring occasionally. Brush sauce over turkey and fruit. Grill about 4 inches above *medium-hot* coals till meat and fruit are hot and well glazed, 5 to 10 minutes. Turn and brush occasionally with sauce. Pass remaining sauce. Makes 4 servings.

A meal from the grill is summer-easy for the cook. ▸
Serve colorful *Fruit-Turkey Kabobs* with grilled slices of buttered French bread for an all-outdoor meal, or serve with kitchen-cooked rice.

Hickory-Smoked Poultry

A smoked turkey is pictured on page 6—

Soak **hickory chunks** and **bark** in **water** for 1 hour. *Or,* dampen **hickory flakes** *or* **chips.** In covered grill have *medium-slow* coals at back and sides of firebox. Center foil drip pan on grill but not directly over coals.

Rinse bird and pat dry; rub cavities with **salt.** Skewer neck skin to back; tie legs securely to tail; twist wing tips under back. Place bird, breast side up, in foil drip pan. Brush bird, *except* duckling, with **cooking oil.** If a meat thermometer is used, insert in center of inside thigh muscle without touching bone.

Sprinkle dampened hickory over coals. Close the hood and grill until meat thermometer registers 185° or until bird is tender. Brush bird often with cooking oil; add dampened hickory about every 20 minutes while grilling.

Hickory-Smoked Chicken: Prepare one 3- to 4- pound whole roasting **chicken.** Grill for 1½ to 2 hours. Makes 4 or 5 servings.

Hickory-Smoked Turkey: Prepare one 12-pound **turkey.** Grill for 3½ to 4½ hours; add more coals, if needed. Let stand 15 minutes before carving. Makes 12 servings.

Hickory-Smoked Duckling: Prepare one 4- to 5- pound domestic **duckling.** Grill for 2¼ to 2½ hours, removing fat. Serves 3 or 4.

Chicken Provençale

> 4 2½- to 3-pound broiler-fryer
>   chickens, halved lengthwise
> Cooking oil
> ½ cup butter, softened
> 2 large tomatoes, peeled, seeded,
>   and finely chopped
> ¼ cup finely chopped onion
> ¼ cup snipped parsley
> ¼ cup dry sherry
> 1 clove garlic, minced
> ½ teaspoon sugar

Brush chicken with oil; sprinkle with salt and pepper. Place, bone side down, over *medium-hot* coals. Grill 25 minutes. Turn; grill 20 minutes more. Meanwhile, combine remaining ingredients (will separate slightly). Brush over chicken; grill till tender, 10 to 15 minutes. Turn twice and brush with sauce. Serves 8.

Rotisserie-Roast Turkey

> 6 tablespoons butter *or*
>   margarine, melted
> ¼ cup dry white wine
> 1 clove garlic, minced
> ½ teaspoon dried rosemary,
>   crushed
> 1 5- to 6-pound frozen boneless
>   turkey roast, thawed

Combine 4 *tablespoons* butter, wine, garlic, and rosemary; let stand several hours at room temperature. Insert spit rod through center of roast; set screws and adjust balance. Insert a meat thermometer in center of roast, not touching spit. Brush roast with remaining butter; season with salt and pepper. Arrange *hot* coals at back and sides of firebox. Center foil drip pan on grill but not directly over coals. Adjust spit in rotisserie; start motor. Allow 2½ to 3 hours total grilling time (thermometer should register 185°). Baste with sauce last 30 minutes. Serves 16 to 18.

Herb-Glazed Chickens

Use a rotisserie for chickens pictured on page 2—

Skewer neck skin to back of two 2½- to 3-pound whole broiler-fryer **chickens.** Slip a 2-foot cord under back of one chicken; bring ends of cord to front, looping around each wing tip. Tie in center of breast so wings can't straighten; leave equal cord ends. Place a holding fork on rod, tines toward point. Insert rod through bird, pressing fork tines firmly into breast meat. Loop an 18-inch cord around tail, then around crossed legs. Tie very tightly to hold bird securely on spit; leave cord ends. Pull together cords attached to wings and to legs; tie tightly. Repeat with second fork and chicken. Add a third holding fork, pressing tines into meat; test balance. Adjust spit in rotisserie and start motor.

Grill chickens over *medium-hot* coals for 1½ to 1¾ hours with barbecue hood lowered *or* about 2 hours on open grill. Meanwhile, combine ½ cup **cooking oil;** ¼ cup light **corn syrup;** ¼ cup finely chopped **onion;** 1 tablespoon **lemon juice;** 1 teaspoon dried **oregano,** crushed; 1 teaspoon **caraway seed;** and ½ teaspoon **salt.** Brush over chickens occasionally during last 30 minutes. Makes 6 to 8 servings.

Honey-Basted Turkey Pieces

Cut one 6- to 7-pound **turkey** into pieces as follows: 2 wings, 2 drumsticks, 2 thighs, 4 breast pieces, and 2 back pieces. Combine ¼ cup **cooking oil,** ¼ cup **soy sauce,** 1 tablespoon **honey,** 1 teaspoon ground **ginger,** 1 teaspoon dry **mustard,** and 1 clove **garlic,** minced. Marinate turkey in soy mixture 2 hours at room temperature or overnight in refrigerator.

Drain turkey pieces, reserving marinade. Place drumsticks, thighs, and breast pieces 6 to 8 inches above *medium-hot* coals. Grill for 30 minutes, turning occasionally. Add wings and back pieces. Grill for 30 minutes, turning occasionally. Baste with marinade and grill until turkey is tender, about 20 minutes more. Makes 10 to 12 servings.

Short-Cut Grilled Chicken

   1 12-ounce jar apricot preserves
   1 8-ounce bottle Russian salad
        dressing with honey (1 cup)
   1 envelope onion soup mix
   3 2½- to 3-pound broiler-fryer
        chickens, cut up

Combine preserves, salad dressing, and soup mix. Grill chicken over *medium* coals till nearly tender, about 45 minutes; turn occasionally. Brush with sauce; grill 15 minutes more, basting occasionally. Makes 12 servings.

Microwave Helps for Outdoor Cooking

To shorten grilling time and still get a barbecue flavor, pre-cook chicken pieces in a countertop microwave oven. For example, a single layer of pieces in a 10x6x2-inch dish that is micro-cooked, covered, about 15 minutes, needs only 10 to 15 minutes on the grill to become tender and "barbecued."

You can also grill several chickens, then micro-heat the leftovers.

Game Hens with Rice Stuffing

   1 6-ounce package long grain and
        wild rice mix
   ¼ cup light raisins
   2 tablespoons butter *or* margarine
   2 tablespoons blanched slivered
        almonds
   ½ teaspoon ground sage
   4 1- to 1½-pound Cornish game
        hens
   ¼ cup butter *or* margarine, melted

Cook rice mix according to package directions; stir in raisins, 2 tablespoons butter, almonds, and sage. Rub cavities of each hen with salt. Skewer neck skin to back. Fill each body cavity with about ¾ cup rice stuffing and cover opening with foil. Tie legs to tail; twist wing tips under back. Brush hens with melted butter. Place hens on foil in center of grill, allowing space between each bird.

Grill over *medium-hot* coals till hens are tender, 1½ to 1¾ hours, brushing occasionally with drippings. Makes 4 servings.

Corn-Stuffed Chicken Breasts

   8 whole chicken breasts
        (3 pounds)
   ¼ cup chopped onion
   ¼ cup chopped celery
   2 tablespoons butter *or* margarine
   1 8¾-ounce can whole kernel
        corn, drained (1 cup)
   1 cup herb-seasoned stuffing mix
   1 slightly beaten egg
   ½ teaspoon poultry seasoning
   ¼ teaspoon salt
   ¼ cup butter *or* margarine,
        melted

Remove bones from chicken breasts, keeping meat in one piece (see page 14). Do *not* remove skin. Sprinkle cut side with salt. In skillet cook onion and celery in 2 tablespoons butter till tender. Add corn, stuffing mix, egg, poultry seasoning, and salt; mix well. Spoon some corn mixture on cut side of each chicken breast. Fold over and skewer or tie closed. Grill over *medium-hot* coals till tender, 30 to 35 minutes, turning often. Brush with melted butter during the last 10 minutes. Makes 8 servings.

Chicken and Vegetable Bundles

4 chicken drumsticks, skinned
4 chicken thighs, skinned
2 large potatoes, peeled and
  cubed
1 8-ounce can sliced carrots,
  drained
1 8-ounce can cut green beans,
  drained
1 small onion, sliced and
  separated into rings
4 tablespoons butter *or* margarine
½ teaspoon dried tarragon,
  crushed
½ teaspoon hickory-smoked salt

Tear off four 18-inch lengths of heavy-duty foil. On each piece of foil, place one chicken leg and one thigh; sprinkle with salt and pepper. Top each serving with a few pieces of potato, carrots, beans, and onion rings. Place 1 tablespoon butter in each bundle; sprinkle each with some of the tarragon and hickory-smoked salt. Bring 4 corners of foil to center; twist securely, allowing room for expansion of steam. Grill over *slow* coals till chicken is tender, about 1 hour. Makes 4 servings.

Hot Turkey Sandwiches

2 cups chopped cooked turkey
1 cup shredded sharp American
  cheese (4 ounces)
1 cup chopped, unpeeled apple
½ cup chopped celery
½ cup mayonnaise
¼ cup toasted slivered almonds
1 tablespoon lemon juice
1 teaspoon curry powder
1 teaspoon salt
⅛ teaspoon pepper
8 individual French rolls

In mixing bowl combine all ingredients except rolls. Cut a thin slice from top of each roll. Hollow out bottoms, leaving ½-inch edges (store bread crumbs for another use). Fill each roll with about ½ cup turkey mixture; replace tops. Wrap each in a 12x12-inch piece of foil, twisting ends securely. Grill over *medium* coals till heated through, 15 to 20 minutes, turning several times. Makes 8 sandwiches.

Basic Broiled Chicken

1 2½- to 3-pound broiler-fryer
  chicken, halved lengthwise *or*
  quartered
Cooking oil *or* melted butter

Preheat broiler. Break wing, hip, and drumstick joints of chicken so bird will remain flat during broiling. Twist wing tips under back. Brush chicken pieces with oil or melted butter and season with salt and pepper.

Place chicken, skin side down, in broiler pan (rack optional—see tip, page 22). Broil with surface of chicken 5 to 6 inches from heat till lightly browned, about 20 minutes. Brush occasionally with oil or butter. Turn chicken skin side up and broil till tender, 15 to 20 minutes more, brushing occasionally with oil or butter. Makes 2 to 4 servings.

Pineapple Hawaiian Chicken

2 2½- to 3-pound broiler-fryer
  chickens, halved lengthwise
  or quartered
Cooking oil
2 tablespoons sugar
1 teaspoon cornstarch
1 8¼-ounce can crushed pineapple
2 tablespoons butter *or* margarine
2 tablespoons soy sauce
1 tablespoon finely chopped onion

Preheat broiler. Break joints of chicken. Brush chicken with oil; season with salt and pepper. Place, skin side down, in broiler pan (rack optional—see tip, page 22). Broil 5 to 6 inches from heat till lightly browned, about 20 minutes. Turn; broil 15 to 20 minutes.

Meanwhile, in small saucepan combine sugar and cornstarch. Stir in crushed pineapple, butter, soy sauce, and chopped onion. Cook and stir till thickened and bubbly; cook 1 minute more. Spoon glaze over chicken the last 5 minutes of broiling time. Serves 4 to 6.

A refreshing blend of pineapple and soy sauce ▸ makes *Pineapple Hawaiian Chicken* a broiler favorite. Quick to prepare, this tropical main dish will soon become a part of your recipe repertoire.

Apple-Spiced Chicken Broil

  1 2½- to 3-pound broiler-fryer
     chicken, quartered
    Cooking oil
  ¼ cup apple jelly
  1 tablespoon lemon juice
  ½ teaspoon ground allspice

Preheat broiler. Break joints of chicken. Brush chicken with oil; season with salt and pepper. Place, skin side down, in broiler pan (rack optional—*see* tip). Broil 5 to 6 inches from heat till lightly browned, about 20 minutes. Turn; broil till tender, 15 to 20 minutes. Meanwhile, in a small saucepan melt jelly over low heat. Stir in lemon juice and allspice. Brush chicken with *half* of the glaze; broil 1 to 2 minutes more. Remove chicken to serving platter; brush with remaining glaze. Makes 4 servings.

Sesame Broiled Chicken

  1 2½- to 3-pound broiler-fryer
     chicken, cut up
    Cooking oil
  2 tablespoons finely chopped onion
  1 small clove garlic, minced
  1 tablespoon butter *or* margarine
  4 teaspoons cornstarch
  1¼ cups water
  2 tablespoons soy sauce
  1½ teaspoons instant chicken
     bouillon granules
  2 tablespoons sesame seed,
     toasted
    Hot cooked noodles *or*
     boiled potatoes

Preheat broiler. Brush chicken pieces with oil and season with salt and pepper. Place, skin side down, in broiler pan (rack optional— see tip). Broil 5 to 6 inches from heat till lightly browned, about 20 minutes. Meanwhile, in small saucepan cook onion and garlic in butter till tender. Blend in cornstarch; add water, soy, and bouillon granules. Cook and stir till thickened and bubbly. Stir in sesame seed.

Turn chicken and broil till tender, 15 to 20 minutes, brushing with some sauce the last 5 minutes. Reheat remaining sauce. Serve chicken with noodles; pass sauce. Serves 4.

Broiled Crab-Chicken Rolls

  6 whole medium chicken breasts
  ¼ cup chopped onion
  ¼ cup chopped celery
  2 tablespoons butter *or* margarine
  4 teaspoons all-purpose flour
    Dash white pepper
  ½ cup milk
  1 7½-ounce can crab meat, drained,
     flaked, and cartilage removed
  ½ cup snipped parsley
  ¼ cup dry sherry
  ¼ cup butter *or* margarine, melted
  1 teaspoon paprika

Remove skin and bones from chicken breasts. Place, boned side up, between two pieces clear plastic wrap. Pound out from center with meat mallet to ⅛-inch thickness. Remove wrap. Season both sides of chicken.

Cook onion and celery in 2 tablespoons butter. Blend in flour, white pepper, and ¼ teaspoon salt. Add milk; cook and stir till bubbly. Stir in crab, parsley, and sherry. Divide crab mixture among chicken pieces. Fold in sides and roll up. Secure with wooden picks. If desired, wrap and chill up to 24 hours.

Preheat broiler. Place chicken in broiler pan (rack optional—see tip). Brush with mixture of melted butter and paprika. Broil 5 to 6 inches from heat about 35 minutes; turn once and brush with butter mixture. Serves 6.

Practical Tips for Broiling Chicken

Broil chicken far enough from the heat to allow golden, even browning—while cooking to the desired doneness. Place chicken on a rack in the broiler pan, then place under unit with surface of chicken 5 to 6 inches from heat. If your broiler compartment does not allow enough distance, remove rack and place chicken directly in broiler pan.

Remember, preheat the broiler unit before cooking, but not the broiler pan.

Chicken Broil with Meat Sauce

¼ pound bulk pork sausage
½ cup finely chopped onion
1 clove garlic, minced
1 8-ounce can tomato sauce
3 tablespoons vinegar
2 tablespoons sugar
1 tablespoon water
½ teaspoon salt
¼ teaspoon dried thyme, crushed
1 2½- to 3-pound broiler-fryer
    chicken, cut up
    Cooking oil
    Hot cooked rice

In skillet brown sausage, onion, and garlic. Stir in next 6 ingredients. Preheat broiler. Brush chicken with oil; season with salt and pepper. Place, skin side down, in broiler pan (rack optional—see tip). Broil 5 to 6 inches from heat till lightly browned, 20 minutes.

Turn chicken; broil 10 minutes. Brush with sauce. Broil 5 to 10 minutes more, brushing occasionally with sauce. Serve with rice; heat and pass remaining sauce. Makes 4 servings.

Fruited Broiled Chicken

1 2½- to 3-pound broiler-fryer
    chicken, quartered
    Cooking oil
1 17-ounce can fruit cocktail
2 teaspoons cornstarch
½ teaspoon ground ginger
¼ teaspoon ground nutmeg
2 tablespoons butter *or* margarine
1 tablespoon lemon juice
1 tablespoon soy sauce

Preheat broiler. Break joints of chicken. Brush chicken with oil; season with salt and pepper. Place, skin side down, in broiler pan (rack optional—see tip). Broil 5 to 6 inches from heat till lightly browned, about 20 minutes. Meanwhile, drain fruit; reserve syrup. In saucepan blend syrup into cornstarch; stir in ginger and nutmeg. Cook and stir till bubbly. Stir in butter, lemon juice, and soy. Turn chicken; broil 10 minutes. Brush with sauce. Broil 5 to 10 minutes, brushing occasionally with sauce. Stir fruit into remaining sauce; heat through. Serve with chicken. Serves 4.

Chicken Teriyaki

1¼ cups water
⅓ cup soy sauce
⅓ cup dry sherry
2 tablespoons sugar
1 small clove garlic, minced (optional)
½ teaspoon ground ginger
6 chicken drumsticks
6 chicken thighs
    Hot cooked rice

In large kettle combine first 6 ingredients; bring to boiling. Add chicken pieces. Cover; simmer till tender, about 30 minutes. Remove chicken from soy mixture. Cool chicken and liquid separately, then place chicken in bowl; pour soy mixture over. Cover; chill at least 4 hours or overnight. (Soy mixture will gel.)

Preheat broiler. Remove fat from soy mixture. Remove chicken; place in broiler pan (rack optional—see tip). Heat soy mixture. Broil chicken 3 inches from heat about 10 minutes; turn and brush each side once with sauce. Serve chicken over rice; pass sauce. Makes 6 servings.

Cumberland-Style Chicken

2 2½- to 3-pound broiler-fryer
    chickens, halved lengthwise
    Cooking oil
1½ teaspoons cornstarch
1 teaspoon dry mustard
⅛ teaspoon ground ginger
½ cup currant jelly
½ of a 6-ounce can frozen orange
    juice concentrate (⅓ cup)
    Dash bottled hot pepper sauce

Preheat broiler. Break joints of chicken. Brush chicken with oil; season with salt and pepper. Place, skin side down, in broiler pan (rack optional—see tip). Broil 5 to 6 inches from heat till lightly browned, about 20 minutes. Turn chicken; broil till tender, 15 to 20 minutes. Meanwhile, in small saucepan combine cornstarch, mustard, and ginger. Stir in remaining ingredients and ¼ cup water. Cook and stir till smooth. Brush chicken with glaze. Broil 2 minutes more; turn and brush each side twice with glaze. Pass remaining glaze. Makes 4 servings.

Classic Casseroles

Chicken-Noodle Casserole

1 8-ounce package frozen noodles
⅓ cup chopped green pepper
⅓ cup chopped onion
2 tablespoons butter *or* margarine
2 tablespoons all-purpose flour
¼ teaspoon dried thyme, crushed
1 11-ounce can condensed Cheddar
 cheese soup
1 cup milk
1½ cups chopped cooked chicken
1 4-ounce can mushroom stems and
 pieces, drained
¼ cup chopped pimiento
¼ cup grated Parmesan cheese
 Parsley sprigs

Cook frozen noodles in 6 cups rapidly boiling water; stir till separated. Cook till tender, 15 to 20 minutes. Drain and set aside.

In saucepan cook green pepper and onion in butter till tender. Blend in flour and thyme. Stir in soup and milk. Cook and stir till thickened and bubbly. Fold in chicken, mushrooms, pimiento, and noodles. Turn into 1½-quart casserole. Sprinkle with cheese. Bake, uncovered, at 350° till heated through, 30 to 35 minutes. Garnish with parsley. Serves 6.

Microwave: Cook noodles as above.

In 2-quart glass casserole cook green pepper and onion in butter in countertop microwave oven till tender, 3½ to 4 minutes; stir twice. Blend in flour and thyme. Stir in soup and milk. Micro-cook, uncovered, till bubbly, 4 to 5 minutes, stirring after each minute. Stir in chicken, mushrooms, pimiento, and noodles. Micro-cook, uncovered, till heated through, 3 to 4 minutes, stirring after 2 minutes. Stir mixture, then sprinkle with cheese. Garnish with parsley and paprika, if desired.

◀ **A crusty-brown batter** seasoned with herb wraps tender pieces of chicken in *Popover Chicken Tarragon*. Whisk this dish from oven to table; spoon *Easy Mushroom Sauce* over each serving.

Popover Chicken Tarragon

1 2½- to 3-pound broiler-fryer
 chicken, cut up
2 tablespoons cooking oil
3 eggs
1½ cups milk
1 tablespoon cooking oil
1½ cups all-purpose flour
¾ to 1 teaspoon dried tarragon,
 crushed
¾ teaspoon salt
 Easy Mushroom Sauce

Brown chicken in 2 tablespoons cooking oil; season with salt and pepper. Place chicken in a well-greased 13x9x2-inch baking dish.

In mixing bowl beat eggs; add milk and 1 tablespoon oil. Stir together the flour, tarragon, and salt. Add to egg mixture. Beat till smooth. Pour over chicken. Bake at 350° till done, 55 to 60 minutes. Spoon Easy Mushroom Sauce over chicken. Makes 4 servings.

Easy Mushroom Sauce: In saucepan cook and stir one 10¾-ounce can condensed **cream of chicken soup;** ⅓ cup **milk;** one 4-ounce can sliced **mushrooms,** drained; and 2 tablespoons snipped **parsley** till bubbly.

Club Chicken Casserole

In saucepan bring 2 cups **chicken broth** and ⅔ cup regular **rice** to boiling. Reduce heat; cook, covered, for 15 minutes. Remove from heat; let stand, covered, 10 minutes.

Cook and drain one 10-ounce package frozen chopped **broccoli.** In saucepan melt 3 tablespoons **butter** *or* **margarine.** Stir in 3 tablespoons all-purpose **flour,** 1½ teaspoons **salt,** and dash **pepper.** Add 2 cups **milk;** cook and stir till thickened and bubbly. Stir in 2 cups cubed cooked **chicken,** the cooked rice, drained broccoli, and one 4-ounce can sliced **mushrooms,** drained. Turn into a 2-quart casserole. Bake, covered, at 350° till heated through, 30 to 35 minutes. Top with ¼ cup toasted slivered **almonds.** Serves 6.

Individual Chicken Pies

½ cup chopped onion
6 tablespoons butter *or* margarine
7 tablespoons all-purpose flour
1 teaspoon salt
¼ teaspoon dried rosemary,
crushed, *or* poultry seasoning
⅛ teaspoon pepper
3 cups chicken broth
3 cups cubed cooked chicken
1 10-ounce package frozen peas and
carrots, cooked and drained
¼ cup chopped pimiento
6 refrigerated biscuits

Cook onion in butter till tender; blend in flour and seasonings. Stir in broth. Cook and stir till thick and bubbly. Add chicken, vegetables, and pimiento; heat till bubbly. Pour into 6 individual casseroles. Quarter biscuits; place 4 pieces atop hot filling in each casserole. Bake at 450° till lightly browned, 8 to 10 minutes. Makes 6 servings.

Carolina Chicken Pie

1 4½- to 5-pound stewing chicken
8 cups water
1 medium onion, sliced
2 celery stalks with leaves
2 parsley sprigs
2 teaspoons salt
¼ teaspoon pepper
3 hard-cooked eggs, chopped
½ cup all-purpose flour
Pastry for 2-crust 9-inch pie

In 5-quart kettle bring first 7 ingredients to boiling. Reduce heat; simmer, covered, till chicken is tender, about 2½ hours. Drain chicken; reserve broth and ¼ cup chicken fat. Strain and refrigerate broth. Cool chicken enough to handle. Remove meat from bones; discard skin and bones. Cube meat; place in 13x9x2-inch baking pan. Sprinkle eggs atop.

In saucepan combine reserved chicken fat and the flour. Stir in *4 cups* of the broth. Cook and stir till bubbly; pour over chicken.

Roll pastry to 14x12-inch rectangle. Place over chicken; seal and flute edges. Cut slits; bake at 375° till filling bubbles and pastry browns, about 45 minutes. Serves 6 to 8.

Chicken Divan

2 10-ounce packages frozen
cut broccoli
1 10¾-ounce can condensed cream
of chicken soup
1 tablespoon lemon juice
1 teaspoon Worcestershire sauce
Dash ground nutmeg
½ cup grated Parmesan cheese
2 cups sliced cooked chicken
½ cup whipping cream
½ cup mayonnaise
Paprika

Cook broccoli; drain well. Arrange in 12x7½x2-inch baking dish. Blend next 4 ingredients; pour *half* over broccoli. Sprinkle with *one-third* of cheese. Top with chicken and remaining soup. Sprinkle with *one-third* of cheese. Bake, uncovered, at 350° till heated through, about 20 minutes.

Whip cream till soft peaks form; fold in mayonnaise. Spread over chicken. Top with remaining cheese and paprika. Broil 4 inches from heat till golden, 2 minutes. Serves 6.

Microwave: *Lay frozen broccoli in 12x7½x2-inch glass baking dish. Add 2 tablespoons water. Cook, covered, in countertop microwave oven 6 minutes; separate pieces. Micro-cook till tender, 4 to 5 minutes. Drain well. Return to dish. Assemble casserole as above. Micro-cook, uncovered, till hot, about 8 minutes, giving dish a half turn once. Whip cream just till soft peaks form; fold in mayonnaise. Spread over chicken. Sprinkle with remaining cheese and paprika. Micro-cook, uncovered, till warm, about 2 minutes.*

Chicken 'n Wild Rice Bake

Cook one 6-ounce package **long grain and wild rice mix** using package directions. Cook ½ pound bulk **pork sausage** and ½ cup chopped **onion.** Drain fat. Stir in 1 cup **chicken broth;** one 4-ounce can **mushroom stems and pieces,** drained; ½ cup chopped **celery with leaves;** and ⅓ cup **cracked wheat cereal.** Cover; simmer 25 minutes. Stir in rice, 2 cups chopped cooked **chicken,** and ½ cup **milk.** Turn into 2-quart casserole. Cover; bake at 375° for 25 to 30 minutes. Serves 6.

Peppy Chicken Lasagna

Cook 4 ounces **lasagna noodles** according to package directions; drain. In saucepan brown 4 ounces bulk **pork sausage;** drain off excess fat. Add 2 cups cubed cooked **chicken;** one 8-ounce can **tomatoes,** cut up; one 8-ounce can **tomato sauce with onion;** ¼ teaspoon dried **oregano,** crushed; and ¼ teaspoon dried **sage,** crushed. Simmer, uncovered, for 10 minutes. Combine 1 beaten **egg;** 1 cup **ricotta** *or* cream-style **cottage cheese,** drained; ¼ cup grated **Parmesan cheese;** and 1 tablespoon snipped **parsley.**

Place *half* of noodles in 10x6x2-inch baking dish. Spread with *half* cheese mixture; top with *half* of one 6-ounce package sliced **mozzarella cheese.** Cover with *half* of chicken mixture. Repeat layers. Bake, covered, at 375° for 35 to 40 minutes. Let stand 10 minutes. Serves 6.

Baked Bean Cassoulet

> 1 pound dry navy beans (2 cups)
> 1 cup chopped celery
> 1 cup chopped carrot
> 2 beef bouillon cubes
> 1 teaspoon salt
> 1 2½- to 3-pound broiler-fryer
>   chicken with giblets, cut up
>
> • • •
>
> ½ pound bulk pork sausage
> 1 cup chopped onion
> 1½ cups tomato juice
> 1 tablespoon Worcestershire sauce

In large kettle boil beans and 8 cups water for 2 minutes. Remove from heat. Do not drain. Cover; let stand 1 hour. Add celery, carrot, bouillon cubes, salt, and chicken neck and giblets. Simmer, covered, for 1 hour.

Shape sausage into small balls; brown in large skillet. Remove sausage; leave drippings. Season chicken; brown in drippings. Remove; set aside. In same skillet cook onion till tender. Stir in tomato juice and Worcestershire. Drain bean mixture, reserving liquid. In 6-quart Dutch oven combine bean mixture, sausage, and tomato mixture. Top with chicken; add 1½ cups bean liquid. Sprinkle with paprika, if desired. Cover; bake at 325° for 1 hour; add bean liquid, if needed. Serves 8.

Chicken Enchiladas

> 1 cup chopped onion
> 1 clove garlic, minced
>   Cooking oil
> 1 tablespoon all-purpose flour
> 1 16-ounce can tomatoes, cut up
> 1 15-ounce can tomato sauce
> 1 4-ounce can green chili peppers,
>   drained, seeded, and chopped
> 1 teaspoon sugar
> 1 teaspoon ground cumin
> ¼ teaspoon salt
> 12 frozen corn tortillas, thawed
>   Chicken Filling
> ¾ cup shredded sharp American cheese
> ¼ cup sliced pitted ripe olives

Cook onion and garlic in *2 tablespoons* oil; stir in flour. Add next 6 ingredients. Cook and stir till thick and bubbly; set aside.

In skillet dip tortillas briefly in small amount of hot oil till limp but not crisp. Drain. Spoon ¼ cup Chicken Filling on each; roll up. Place in 13x9x2-inch baking dish. Pour tomato mixture over all. Bake, covered, at 350° about 15 minutes. Uncover; bake till heated through, about 15 minutes. Top with cheese and bake till cheese melts. Top with olives. Makes 6 servings.

Chicken Filling: Combine 2 cups chopped cooked **chicken,** ¾ cup shredded sharp **American cheese,** ¼ cup finely chopped **onion,** ¼ cup chopped pitted **ripe olives,** and ¾ teaspoon **salt.**

 ### Seasoning Poultry with Herbs and Spices

Change the seasonings and create a new dish. Start with ½ teaspoon for four servings, then taste before adding more.

On the bird: Basil, cayenne, chervil, marjoram, paprika, rosemary, savory, sesame seed, thyme

In the sauce: Allspice, dill, curry powder, mace, nutmeg, parsley, tarragon

For the stuffing: Basil, celery seed, oregano, poultry seasoning, sage

Chicken-Cheese Strata

Trim crusts from 2 slices **bread;** cube bread. Divide between two 1-cup casseroles. Mix one 10¾-ounce can condensed **chicken noodle soup** and 2 beaten **eggs;** pour over bread. Cover; chill several hours or overnight. Sprinkle with ¼ cup shredded sharp **American cheese.** Bake at 325° till set, 35 to 40 minutes. Serves 2.

Scalloped Chicken and Potatoes

    3 medium potatoes, peeled and
        thinly sliced (3 cups)
    2 carrots, thinly sliced (1 cup)
    ½ cup chopped onion
    ¼ cup chopped celery
    2 cups chopped cooked chicken
    3 tablespoons all-purpose flour
    1 teaspoon salt
    2 cups milk
    ⅓ cup hot-style catsup
    1 teaspoon Worcestershire sauce

Combine vegetables; carefully stir in chicken. In saucepan combine flour, salt, and dash pepper; blend in milk. Stir in catsup and Worcestershire. Cook and stir till bubbly. Stir into vegetables. Turn into 2-quart casserole. Bake, covered, at 375° till potatoes are tender, about 1½ hours. Makes 6 servings.

Microwave: Use above ingredients except increase flour to ¼ cup. In 2-quart glass casserole combine vegetables and ½ cup water. Cook, covered, in countertop microwave oven till crisp-tender, 9 to 10 minutes; stir every 3 minutes. Drain. Stir in chicken; set aside. In 4-cup glass measure combine ¼ cup flour, salt, and dash pepper. Blend in milk; stir in catsup and Worcestershire. Micro-cook, uncovered, for 2 minutes; stir. Micro-cook till thickened and bubbly, about 3 minutes; stir every 30 seconds. Carefully stir into vegetables. Micro-cook, uncovered, till heated through, about 5 minutes, stirring once.

◄ **These popular main dishes** bake while you relax. Delight Italian sausage fans with *Chicken-Zucchini Bake,* or serve *Chicken Wings with Potatoes* (see recipe, page 13) for a crisp meal without frying.

Chicken-Zucchini Bake

    4 ounces bulk Italian sausage
    4 medium zucchini (1½ pounds)
    ½ cup grated Parmesan cheese
    ½ cup fine dry bread crumbs
    1½ cups chopped cooked chicken
    1 tablespoon snipped parsley
    ½ teaspoon salt
    ⅛ teaspoon pepper
    3 eggs, separated
    ¼ cup milk
    1 tablespoon butter, melted
        Paprika

Brown sausage; drain off fat. Remove ends from zucchini. Cook whole zucchini in small amount of boiling water till crisp-tender, about 8 minutes; drain. Cut 3 thin slices from one zucchini; set aside. Finely chop remainder.

In large bowl combine cheese and crumbs. Reserve 2 tablespoons; set aside. Toss remaining crumbs with sausage, chopped zucchini, chicken, parsley, salt, and pepper. Beat egg whites till stiff peaks form. Beat egg yolks and milk till blended; stir into chicken mixture. Fold in beaten egg whites. Turn into 8x1½-inch round baking dish. Combine reserved crumbs and melted butter; sprinkle over casserole. Sprinkle with paprika. Bake, uncovered, at 325° till set, 35 to 40 minutes. Garnish with reserved zucchini slices. Makes 4 or 5 servings.

Chicken and Stuffing Scallop

Prepare ½ of an 8-ounce package **herb-seasoned stuffing mix** (2 cups) according to package directions for dry stuffing. Spread in a 10x6x2-inch baking dish; top with 2 cups chopped cooked **chicken** or **turkey.** Melt ¼ cup **butter;** blend in ¼ cup all-purpose **flour,** ⅛ teaspoon **salt,** and dash **pepper.** Add 2 cups **chicken broth;** cook and stir till bubbly. Stir moderate amount of hot mixture into 3 beaten **eggs;** return to hot mixture. Pour over chicken; bake at 325° till set, about 35 minutes. Let stand 5 minutes. Top with sliced **green olives;** serve with Pimiento Sauce. Serves 6.

Pimiento Sauce: Heat one 11-ounce can condensed **Cheddar cheese soup,** ½ cup **milk,** and 2 tablespoons chopped **pimiento.**

Wine and Wild Rice Casserole

1 6-ounce package long grain and
    wild rice mix
½ cup chopped onion
½ cup chopped celery
2 tablespoons butter *or* margarine
1 10¾-ounce can condensed cream
    of mushroom soup
½ cup dairy sour cream
⅓ cup dry white wine
½ teaspoon curry powder
2 cups cubed cooked chicken *or* turkey
¼ cup snipped parsley

Prepare rice mix according to package directions. Meanwhile, in saucepan cook onion and celery in butter till tender but not brown. Blend in soup, sour cream, wine, and curry. Stir in chicken and cooked rice; turn into 12x7½x2-inch baking dish. Bake, uncovered, at 350° for 35 to 40 minutes. Stir before serving; garnish with parsley. Makes 4 to 6 servings.

Microwave: Prepare rice mix according to package directions on top of the range. Meanwhile, place onion, celery, and butter in a 2-quart glass casserole. Cook, covered, in a countertop microwave oven till tender, 2 to 2½ minutes. Blend in soup, sour cream, wine, and curry. Stir in chicken and cooked rice. Microcook, covered, till heated through, 8 to 10 minutes, giving casserole a half turn after 5 minutes. Garnish with parsley.

Chicken and Rice Stew

Place one cut-up 2½- to 3-pound broiler-fryer **chicken** in large skillet. Add 1 cup **water,** ¼ cup chopped **onion,** 1 teaspoon **celery salt,** and dash **pepper.** Cover; simmer till chicken is almost tender, 20 to 30 minutes. Remove chicken. Measure broth; add **water** to make 2 cups liquid. Return to skillet. Stir in one 15½-ounce can cut **green beans,** drained; one 10¾-ounce can condensed **cream of mushroom soup;** 1 cup uncooked regular **rice;** ½ cup **milk;** ½ cup grated **Parmesan cheese;** ¼ cup **mayonnaise** *or* **salad dressing;** 2 tablespoons chopped **pimiento;** and ¼ teaspoon **Worcestershire sauce.** Add chicken; cover and simmer till rice is done, about 30 minutes. Sprinkle with **paprika.** Makes 4 to 6 servings.

Chicken Stroganoff

In plastic bag combine ¼ cup all-purpose **flour,** 1 teaspoon **salt,** ¼ teaspoon **paprika,** and ⅛ teaspoon **pepper.** Using one cut-up 2½- to 3-pound broiler-fryer **chicken,** shake pieces in flour, a few at a time, to coat evenly. In skillet brown chicken in ¼ cup **butter** about 10 minutes; turn often. Transfer to a 3-quart casserole.

In skillet combine one 13¾-ounce can **chicken broth;** two 4-ounce cans **mushroom stems and pieces,** drained; 1 medium **onion,** chopped; and 1 clove **garlic,** minced. Heat to boiling; pour over chicken. Cover; bake at 350° for 30 minutes. Stir in 4 ounces uncooked **noodles** (3 cups); bake, covered, 30 minutes. Remove chicken to platter; stir some noodles into 1 cup dairy **sour cream;** add to remaining noodles. Serve with chicken. Serves 4.

Chicken Puff Casserole

¼ cup butter *or* margarine
¼ cup all-purpose flour
½ teaspoon salt
    Dash pepper
1½ cups milk
1 cup chicken broth
2 cups cubed cooked chicken
    or turkey
1 cup frozen peas, cooked and
    drained
2 tablespoons chopped pimiento
3 eggs, separated
½ cup all-purpose flour
1 teaspoon baking powder
½ teaspoon paprika
½ teaspoon salt
½ cup milk
1 tablespoon cooking oil

Melt butter; blend in ¼ cup flour, ½ teaspoon salt, and pepper. Add 1½ cups milk and broth. Cook and stir till bubbly. Add chicken, peas, and pimiento; heat. Cover and keep hot.

Beat egg whites till stiff peaks form. Beat egg yolks till thick. Combine ½ cup flour, baking powder, paprika, and ½ teaspoon salt. Add to yolks alternately with ½ cup milk and oil. Fold in whites. Turn chicken mixture into 11x7½x1½-inch baking pan. Top with batter. Bake at 425° for 20 to 25 minutes. Serves 4 or 5.

Turkey Pie in a Skillet

⅓ cup chopped celery
6 tablespoons butter *or* margarine
2 cups herb-seasoned stuffing mix
⅔ cup water
3 beaten eggs
1 5⅓-ounce can evaporated milk
  (⅔ cup)
1 single serving-size envelope
  cream of mushroom soup mix
2 tablespoons finely chopped
  onion
  Dash pepper
3 cups finely chopped *or* ground
  cooked turkey
1 cup shredded Swiss cheese
2 tablespoons snipped parsley
  Instant Mushroom Sauce

Cook celery in butter till tender. Add stuffing mix and water; toss to coat. In bowl combine eggs, milk, soup mix, onion, and pepper. Stir in turkey; turn into well-greased 8-inch skillet; sprinkle with cheese. Top with stuffing mixture. Cover; cook over medium-low heat for 10 to 15 minutes. Sprinkle with parsley. Let stand 5 minutes. Serve with Instant Mushroom Sauce. Makes 4 to 6 servings.

Instant Mushroom Sauce: Dissolve 2 single serving-size envelopes **cream of mushroom soup mix** in 1 cup boiling **water**.

Poultry—Economical and Nutritious

Include poultry in your meals often to stretch your food budget. Not only are chicken and turkey low in cost, but they are high in protein and other nutrients. Because of their low caloric and fat contents, chicken and turkey are useful in reducing and other special diets.

Choose a larger chicken or turkey for a greater proportion of meat to bone, and more value for the money. The leftovers will be great in soups, salads, sandwiches, and casseroles (see page 92).

Turkey-Mushroom Quiche

1 cup finely chopped cooked
  turkey *or* chicken
1 4½-ounce jar sliced mushrooms,
  drained
1 9-inch baked pastry shell,
  cooled
¾ cup shredded American cheese
1 10¾-ounce can condensed
  cream of shrimp soup
¼ cup milk
4 beaten eggs

Arrange turkey and mushrooms in cooled baked pastry shell; sprinkle with cheese. In small saucepan combine soup and milk; heat just to boiling, stirring constantly. Gradually stir into eggs. Pour soup mixture over cheese. Bake, uncovered, at 325° till knife inserted off-center comes out clean, 40 to 45 minutes. Let stand 10 minutes. Makes 6 servings.

Chicken Jambalaya

1 2½- to 3-pound broiler-fryer
  chicken, cut up
1 cup chopped onion
1 clove garlic, minced
2 tablespoons cooking oil
1 28-ounce can tomatoes, cut up
1 teaspoon salt
  Few drops bottled hot pepper
  sauce
1 bay leaf
½ pound frozen shelled shrimp *or*
  one 4½-ounce can shrimp,
  drained
1 cup regular rice
1 cup sliced celery
2 tablespoons snipped parsley

Season chicken with a little salt and pepper. In large skillet brown chicken, onion, and garlic in hot oil about 15 minutes. Add undrained tomatoes, salt, pepper sauce, and bay leaf. Heat to boiling. Cover; reduce heat. Simmer for 30 minutes. Spoon off fat. Add shrimp, rice, celery, and parsley, making sure all rice is covered with liquid. Cover and simmer till rice is tender, about 30 minutes longer. Remove bay leaf. Garnish with parsley sprig, if desired. Makes 6 servings.

Oven and Range-Top Dishes

Chicken in a Pot

1 teaspoon salt
¼ teaspoon dried thyme, crushed
¼ teaspoon dried marjoram,
    crushed
¼ teaspoon celery salt
¼ teaspoon pepper
1 3-pound whole broiler-fryer
    chicken

Use a glazed or unglazed ceramic chicken pot. Season pot, if necessary, according to the manufacturer's directions. Combine salt, thyme, marjoram, celery salt, and pepper. Rub chicken with seasonings. Rub cavity of bird with additional salt. Skewer neck skin to back. Tie legs to tail; twist wings under back. Place chicken in pot, breast side up. Cover tightly and place in *unheated* oven. Turn on oven to 400° and bake till chicken is tender, about 1½ hours. (Very heavy or thick pots may require more baking time.) Makes 4 servings.

German-Style Chicken

1 2½- to 3-pound broiler-fryer
    chicken, cut up
2 tablespoons cooking oil *or*
    shortening
1 cup water
2 tablespoons brown sugar
2 tablespoons vinegar
1½ teaspoons salt
¼ teaspoon pepper
1 medium head cabbage, cut in
    eight wedges (1½ pounds)
½ teaspoon caraway seed

In 12-inch skillet brown chicken pieces in hot oil over medium heat about 15 minutes. Combine water, brown sugar, vinegar, salt, and pepper; pour over chicken. Cover and simmer for 20 minutes. Add cabbage wedges and caraway seed. Cover and cook till chicken and cabbage are tender, about 15 minutes longer. Arrange chicken and cabbage on serving platter; spoon pan juices over. Makes 4 servings.

Chicken Chow Mein

2 whole large chicken breasts,
    skinned and boned
2 tablespoons butter *or* margarine
1½ cups sliced celery
1 cup chopped onion
1 cup chicken broth
¼ cup soy sauce
2 tablespoons cornstarch
¼ teaspoon ground ginger
1 16-ounce can bean sprouts,
    drained
1 5-ounce can water chestnuts,
    drained and halved
Chow mein noodles

Cut chicken in ½-inch squares. In skillet brown chicken on all sides in butter about 5 minutes. Add celery, onion, and broth. Cover; simmer till chicken is cooked and vegetables are crisp-tender, about 10 minutes. Combine soy, cornstarch, and ginger; blend into chicken. Cook and stir till bubbly. Stir in bean sprouts and water chestnuts. Cover and cook, stirring occasionally, till heated through, about 5 minutes. Serve over noodles. Makes 4 servings.

*Microwave: Use above ingredients **except** increase cornstarch to 3 tablespoons. Cut chicken in ½-inch squares. In 2-quart glass casserole melt butter in countertop microwave oven 30 to 40 seconds. Add chicken, celery, onion, and broth. Micro-cook, covered, till chicken is cooked, about 10 minutes; stir after 5 minutes. Combine soy, 3 tablespoons cornstarch, and ginger; blend into chicken. Micro-cook, uncovered, till bubbly, 2½ to 3 minutes, stirring after each minute. Stir in bean sprouts and water chestnuts. Micro-cook, uncovered, till heated through, about 1½ minutes, stirring twice. Serve over chow mein noodles.*

Delicately seasoned with herbs, *Chicken in a Pot* ▶ becomes beautifully browned, yet remains moist and tender. The secret lies in snugly fitting the bird into a ceramic chicken pot for baking.

Lemon-Sweet Chicken

¼ cup all-purpose flour
1 2½- to 3-pound broiler-fryer
    chicken, cut up
2 tablespoons cooking oil
1 6-ounce can frozen lemonade
    concentrate, thawed
½ cup water
3 tablespoons brown sugar
3 tablespoons catsup
1 tablespoon vinegar
1 tablespoon cornstarch
    Hot cooked rice

In plastic bag combine flour and 1 teaspoon salt. Add chicken pieces, a few at a time; shake to coat. In skillet brown chicken in hot oil 15 minutes. Spoon off fat. Blend lemonade concentrate, ½ cup water, brown sugar, catsup, and vinegar. Pour over chicken. Bring to boiling; cover and simmer till tender, 45 to 50 minutes. Remove chicken to platter; keep warm.

Skim fat from pan juices. Measure juices; add water, if needed, to make 1¼ cups liquid. Return to pan. Blend 1 tablespoon cold water into cornstarch. Stir into pan juices. Cook and stir till thickened and bubbly. Pass sauce with chicken; serve over rice. Makes 4 servings.

Crockery Cooker: Coat and brown chicken as above. Transfer chicken pieces to an electric slow crockery cooker. Blend concentrate, ½ cup water, brown sugar, catsup, and vinegar; pour over chicken. Cover and cook on high-heat setting till tender, 3 to 3½ hours. Remove chicken to platter; keep warm. Prepare sauce in a saucepan as above; serve as above.

Baked Orange-Rum Chicken

In small saucepan combine ¼ cup **rum,** 2 tablespoons **butter** or **margarine,** 1 tablespoon **brown sugar,** 1 tablespoon frozen **orange juice concentrate,** ½ teaspoon **salt,** ⅛ teaspoon **pepper,** and ⅛ teaspoon ground **ginger.** Heat and stir to dissolve sugar. Using one cut-up 2½- to 3-pound broiler-fryer **chicken,** brush pieces with some of the rum mixture. Arrange chicken, skin side up, in large shallow baking pan. Bake, uncovered, at 375° for 50 to 60 minutes, basting once during baking and again just before serving with rum mixture. Makes 4 servings.

Chicken with Apples

1 2½- to 3-pound broiler-fryer
    chicken, quartered or cut up
¼ cup butter or margarine
1 teaspoon salt
¼ teaspoon pepper
1 cup apple cider or apple juice
1 teaspoon lemon juice
4 tart cooking apples, peeled
    and sliced (3 cups)
1 tablespoon cornstarch
1 tablespoon brown sugar
¼ teaspoon ground cinnamon

In skillet brown chicken slowly in butter about 10 minutes, turning often. Remove from heat; drain off fat. Sprinkle chicken with salt and pepper. Add cider and lemon juice. Cover; simmer for 25 minutes. Add apples; simmer till just tender, 5 to 10 minutes longer. Remove chicken and apples to platter; keep warm. Skim fat from pan juices. Measure juices; add water, if needed, to make 1 cup. In saucepan blend cornstarch, brown sugar, and cinnamon. Stir in juices. Cook and stir till thickened and bubbly. Season to taste with salt and pepper. Spoon some sauce over chicken and apples; pass remaining sauce. Makes 4 servings.

 Cook Frozen Chicken Pieces Without Thawing

For best results, rinse chicken pieces and pat dry. Tightly wrap pieces individually in plastic bags, then overwrap in moisture-vaporproof material. (Wrap backs together to use in soups.) Seal, label, and freeze up to 6 months.

Save time and effort when cooking the frozen chicken—don't thaw it! When you're ready to cook, remove as many pieces from the freezer as you need. Run under cold water several minutes to loosen plastic. For skillet dishes, simply brown chicken 5 minutes longer, then finish cooking. For oven dishes, bake frozen chicken an extra 15 to 20 minutes.

Stewed Chicken

    1 5- to 6-pound stewing chicken,
        cut up, *or* 2 3-pound broiler-
        fryer chickens, cut up
    4 stalks celery with leaves,
        cut up
    1 carrot, sliced
    1 small onion, cut up
    2 sprigs parsley
    1 bay leaf
    2 teaspoons salt
    ¼ teaspoon pepper

Place chicken in a large kettle; add water to cover (about 8 cups). Add remaining ingredients. Cover; bring to boiling. Simmer till chicken is tender, about 1 hour for broiler-fryers *or* 2 to 2½ hours for stewing chicken. Remove chicken; strain broth. When cool enough to handle, cut meat from bones; discard skin and bones. Store meat and broth separately in covered containers; chill. Makes 5 cups cooked chicken.

Crockery Cooker: Use above ingredients except substitute one 3½- to 4-pound stewing chicken for birds listed; use only 4 cups water and 1 teaspoon salt. Combine all ingredients in electric slow crockery cooker. Cover; cook on low-heat setting 8 hours or high-heat setting 4 hours. Store. Makes 4 cups cooked chicken.

Chicken and Homemade Noodles

Prepare noodles: Combine 2 beaten **eggs**, ¼ cup **milk**, and ¾ teaspoon **salt**. Add enough all-purpose **flour** to make a stiff dough (about 2 cups). Divide dough in half. Roll very thin on floured surface; let stand 20 minutes. Roll up loosely; slice ¼ inch wide. Unroll; cut into desired lengths. Let dry 2 hours.

    Meanwhile, place one cut-up 5- to 6-pound stewing **chicken** in large kettle. Add **water** to cover (about 8 cups); 1 medium **onion**, chopped; 4 teaspoons **salt**; and ¼ teaspoon **pepper**. Cover; bring to boiling. Simmer for 2 to 2½ hours. Remove chicken; cool. Remove meat from bones; discard skin and bones. Bring broth to boiling; add noodles and 3 **carrots**, thinly sliced. Cover and simmer 10 minutes. Add chicken. Blend ¼ cup cold **water** into 2 tablespoons all-purpose **flour**; add to broth. Cook and stir till slightly thickened. Serves 6 to 8.

Chicken and Dumplings

Home cooking at its best, pictured on page 4—

    Stewed Chicken
    ½ teaspoon ground sage (optional)
    1 cup all-purpose flour
    2 teaspoons baking powder
    ½ teaspoon salt
    2 tablespoons snipped parsley
    1 egg
    ¼ cup milk
    2 tablespoons butter, melted
    1 cup cold water
    ½ cup all-purpose flour
    1½ teaspoons salt
    ⅛ teaspoon pepper

Prepare Stewed Chicken *except* add sage to cooking liquid, if desired.

    Prepare dumplings when chicken is almost tender: Stir together 1 cup flour, baking powder, and ½ teaspoon salt; add parsley. Stir together egg, milk, and melted butter. Add to flour mixture, stirring just till blended. Drop dough from tablespoon directly onto chicken in boiling broth. Cover tightly; return to boiling. Reduce heat; *do not lift cover.* Simmer 12 to 15 minutes. Remove dumplings and chicken to platter; keep warm. Strain broth.

    Thicken broth for gravy: In saucepan bring *4 cups* broth to boiling. Stir cold water into ½ cup flour; gradually add to broth, mixing well. Cook and stir till thickened and bubbly. Season with 1½ teaspoons salt and pepper. Pour over chicken and dumplings. Serves 6 to 8.

Chicken with Artichokes

Drain and quarter one 6-ounce jar marinated **artichoke hearts**, reserving liquid. Sprinkle 4 whole medium **chicken breasts** with ½ teaspoon **salt** and dash **pepper**. In large skillet cook chicken in reserved liquid till golden brown, about 15 minutes. Skim off *excess* fat. Push chicken to one side of skillet. Add one 10¾-ounce can condensed **cream of mushroom soup**, one 8-ounce can **tomato sauce**, quartered artichokes, and 1 teaspoon **sugar**. Stir to combine. Rearrange chicken in skillet; cover and simmer 30 to 35 minutes, stirring occasionally. Serve chicken and artichokes over hot cooked **rice**. Pass sauce. Makes 4 servings.

Fruited Chicken Breasts

¼ teaspoon grated orange peel
½ cup orange juice
1 tablespoon chopped onion
1 teaspoon instant chicken
    bouillon granules
3 whole medium chicken breasts,
    skinned and halved lengthwise
  Paprika
1 tablespoon cornstarch
½ cup seedless green grapes,
    halved

In skillet combine the first 4 ingredients. Add chicken; sprinkle with paprika, salt, and pepper. Cover and simmer till chicken is tender, 30 to 35 minutes. Remove chicken to platter; keep warm. Measure pan juices; add water, if needed, to make ¾ cup. Return to pan. Blend 1 tablespoon cold water into cornstarch; stir into juices. Cook and stir till thickened and bubbly. Add grapes; cook 1 to 2 minutes. Spoon some sauce over chicken; pass remainder. Garnish with orange slices, if desired. Makes 6 servings.

Microwave: In 12x7½x2-inch glass baking dish combine first 4 ingredients. Add chicken; sprinkle with paprika, salt, and pepper. Cover with waxed paper. Cook in countertop microwave oven for 12 minutes; rearrange chicken after 6 minutes. Remove chicken; keep warm. Measure pan juices; add water to make ¾ cup. Blend 1 tablespoon cold water into cornstarch; stir into juices. Micro-cook till bubbly, about 2 minutes; stir after 1 minute. Add grapes; micro-cook 30 seconds. Serve as above.

Chicken Cacciatore

In skillet brown one cut-up 2½- to 3-pound broiler-fryer **chicken** in 2 tablespoons **cooking oil**. Remove chicken. In same skillet cook 2 medium **onions,** sliced, and 2 cloves **garlic,** minced, till tender. Return chicken to skillet. Combine one 16-ounce can **tomatoes;** one 8-ounce can **tomato sauce;** 1 teaspoon dried **oregano** *or* basil, crushed; 1 teaspoon **salt;** ½ teaspoon **celery seed;** 1 or 2 **bay leaves;** and ¼ teaspoon **pepper.** Pour over chicken. Cover; simmer 30 minutes. Stir in ¼ cup dry **white wine.** Cook, uncovered, 15 minutes; turn often. Remove bay leaves; skim fat. Serves 4.

A dieter's delight, *Fruited Chicken Breasts* can be made on the range-top or in your countertop microwave oven. Each serving contains only 206 calories.

Chicken Fricassee

½ cup all-purpose flour
1 3½-pound broiler-fryer
    chicken, cut up
2 tablespoons shortening
½ cup chopped celery
¼ cup chopped onion
1 10¾-ounce can condensed
    cream of mushroom soup
¾ cup water
2 tablespoons chopped pimiento
  Hot cooked rice

In plastic bag combine flour, 1 teaspoon salt, and ⅛ teaspoon pepper. Add chicken pieces, a few at a time; shake to coat. In skillet brown chicken in the shortening; transfer to 3-quart casserole. In same skillet cook celery and onion till tender but not brown. Drain fat. Stir in soup, water, and pimiento; pour over chicken. Cover; bake at 350° till tender, about 1 hour. Serve with rice. Makes 4 or 5 servings.

Chicken and Cranberries

Cut 3 whole large **chicken breasts** in half lengthwise. In paper or plastic bag combine ⅓ cup all-purpose **flour**, 1½ teasoons **salt**, ½ teaspoon **paprika**, and dash **garlic salt**. Add chicken pieces, a few at a time; shake to coat evenly. In a large skillet brown chicken pieces slowly in ¼ cup **butter** *or* **margarine** about 10 minutes, turning often to brown evenly.

Combine one 8-ounce can whole **cranberry sauce** and 1 cup dry **white wine**; pour mixture over chicken in skillet. Cover and simmer till chicken is tender, 35 to 45 minutes. Pass pan juices with chicken. Makes 6 servings.

Italian Chicken over Spaghetti

    3½ pounds broiler-fryer chicken
       pieces
    1 15-ounce can tomato sauce
    1 10¾-ounce can condensed tomato
       soup
    ⅔ cup milk (½ soup can)
    1 6-ounce can tomato paste
    2 cloves garlic, minced
    2 teaspoons dried oregano,
       crushed
    1 teaspoon dried basil, crushed
       Dash salt
       Dash pepper
    ½ cup grated Parmesan cheese
    4 slices mozzarella cheese
       (6 ounces)
       Hot cooked spaghetti

Place chicken in a roasting pan. Combine next 9 ingredients; pour over chicken. Cover and bake at 375° for 1 hour. Sprinkle with Parmesan cheese; top with mozzarella slices. Bake, covered, till chicken is tender, about 10 minutes. Remove chicken; keep warm. Blend cheeses remaining in pan into sauce. Serve chicken and sauce over spaghetti. Serves 6.

Crockery Cooker: Place chicken in an electric slow crockery cooker. Combine next 9 ingredients; pour over chicken. Cover and cook on low-heat setting for 8 hours. Meanwhile, shred mozzarella cheese. Turn cooker to high-heat setting. Remove chicken; keep warm. Stir cheeses into sauce. Cook, covered, for 10 minutes. Serve chicken and sauce over spaghetti.

Garlic Chicken

    ¼ cup all-purpose flour
    1 teaspoon salt
    ¼ teaspoon pepper
    1 2½- to 3-pound broiler-fryer
       chicken, cut up
    2 tablespoons cooking oil or
       shortening
    3 or 4 cloves garlic, minced
    1 teaspoon instant beef bouillon
       granules
    1 cup boiling water
    ½ cup cold water
    2 tablespoons all-purpose flour

In paper or plastic bag combine ¼ cup flour, salt, and pepper. Add chicken, a few pieces at a time; shake to coat. Brown chicken in hot oil about 15 minutes. Add garlic; cook 5 minutes longer. Spoon off fat. Dissolve beef bouillon granules in 1 cup boiling water; add to skillet. Reduce heat. Cover and simmer till chicken is tender, 35 to 40 minutes. Remove the chicken to a serving platter and keep warm.

Measure pan juices; add water, if needed, to make 1 cup. Blend ½ cup cold water into 2 tablespoons flour. In saucepan combine pan juices and flour mixture. Cook and stir till thickened and bubbly. Season to taste with salt and pepper. Pass sauce with chicken; serve over hot cooked noodles, if desired. Makes 4 servings.

Chicken Loaf

Combine 2 beaten **eggs**, one 5⅓-ounce can **evaporated milk**, and ⅓ cup **chicken broth**. Stir in 1½ cups soft **bread crumbs** (about 2 slices bread); ⅔ cup chopped **celery**; ¼ cup chopped **pimiento**; ¾ teaspoon **salt**; dash **pepper**; dash dried **rosemary**, crushed; dash dried **marjoram**, crushed; and dash ground **nutmeg**. Add 4 cups coarsely ground cooked **chicken** (one 4- to 5-pound stewing chicken); mix well. Line the bottom of a greased 8½x4½x 2½-inch loaf dish with foil; grease the foil. Turn chicken mixture into dish. Bake at 350° till center is firm, about 45 minutes. Invert onto platter; remove foil. Pass Mushroom Sauce. Serves 6.

Mushroom Sauce: In saucepan combine one 10¾-ounce can condensed **cream of mushroom soup** and ⅓ cup **milk**; heat through.

Salads, Soups, and Sandwiches

Mexican Chef's Salad

6 cups torn lettuce
1 cup shredded carrot (2 carrots)
1 cup chopped celery (2 stalks
   celery)
1 cup cooked chicken cut in
   julienne strips
1 cup fully cooked ham cut in
   julienne strips
2 tomatoes, chopped
3 tablespoons sliced green onion
   with tops
• • •
2 cups shredded sharp American
   cheese (8 ounces)
⅔ cup milk
3 tablespoons chopped, seeded
   canned green chili peppers
3 tablespoons sliced pitted ripe
   olives
2 cups corn chips

In large salad bowl combine lettuce, carrot, and celery. Arrange chicken, ham, tomatoes, and green onion atop. In heavy saucepan combine cheese and milk. Cook and stir over low heat till cheese is melted and mixture is smooth. Stir in chilies and olives. Just before serving, pour sauce over salad. Toss lightly. Pass corn chips to sprinkle atop. Makes 6 servings.
   Note: If desired, cheese sauce may be made ahead and served cold. Increase milk in sauce to 1 cup. Chill till serving time.

Chicken and Brown Rice Salad

In mixing bowl combine ¾ cup **mayonnaise** *or* **salad dressing** and 1 tablespoon **lemon juice**. Add 2 cups chopped cooked **chicken**; 2 cups cooked **brown rice** (⅔ cup uncooked); 1 cup sliced **celery**; ¼ cup sliced **almonds**, toasted; 2 tablespoons sliced **water chestnuts**; 1 tablespoon sliced **green onion** with tops; ¼ teaspoon **salt**; and dash **pepper**. Mix lightly. Chill at least 4 hours. Serve in 6 **lettuce cups**; garnish with more toasted **almonds**. Makes 6 servings.

Chicken Salad in Tomatoes

Combine 2 cups chopped cooked **chicken** *or* **turkey**, 1 cup diced fully cooked **ham**, and 1 tablespoon finely chopped **onion**; blend in ¼ cup **French salad dressing**. Cover and chill at least 1 hour. Combine ½ cup **mayonnaise** *or* **salad dressing** and 1 tablespoon prepared **mustard**. Add with ½ cup chopped **celery** to chicken mixture; toss lightly. Season to taste.
   Place 6 chilled **tomatoes** stem end down. Cut each, not quite through, into 6 wedges. Spread wedges apart; sprinkle with **salt**. Fill with salad. Serve on **lettuce**; garnish with **parsley** *or* **ripe olives**. Makes 6 servings.

Chicken-Macaroni Molds

1 3-ounce package lemon-flavored
   gelatin
2 tablespoons wine vinegar
1 tablespoon chopped onion
1 teaspoon salt
   Dash pepper
⅓ cup mayonnaise
1 cup chopped cooked chicken
   or turkey
1 cup cooked macaroni
½ cup chopped celery
   Lettuce
   Tomato wedges

Dissolve gelatin in 1 cup boiling water. Stir in vinegar, onion, salt, pepper, and ½ cup cold water. Gradually stir gelatin mixture into mayonnaise; beat till smooth. Chill till partially set. Fold in chicken, macaroni, and celery. Turn into six ½-cup molds. Chill till firm, 3 to 4 hours. Unmold onto lettuce-lined plates. Garnish with tomato. Makes 6 servings.

An attractive combination of vegetables, ham, and ❯ chicken makes *Mexican Chef's Salad* a welcome main dish. Serve it with hot cheese sauce flavored with chilies and olives, then sprinkle with corn chips.

Chicken-Pineapple Bowl

The salad has only 201 calories per serving—leftover dressing's just 6 calories a tablespoon

2½ cups cubed cooked chicken
   or turkey
2 cups drained canned pineapple
   chunks (juice pack)
1 cup green pepper strips
½ cup sliced water chestnuts
   Lettuce leaves
¾ cup Zesty Salad Dressing

In salad bowl arrange chicken or turkey, pineapple chunks, green pepper, and water chestnuts on lettuce leaves. Add Zesty Salad Dressing and toss lightly. Makes 4 servings.

Zesty Salad Dressing: In small saucepan combine 1 tablespoon **cornstarch,** 1 teaspoon **sugar,** and 1 teaspoon dry **mustard;** gradually stir in 1 cup cold **water.** Cook, stirring constantly, over medium heat till thickened and bubbly. Remove from heat. Cover surface with waxed paper. Cool 10 to 15 minutes. Remove the waxed paper; stir in ¼ cup **vinegar,** ¼ cup **catsup,** 1 teaspoon prepared **horseradish,** 1 teaspoon **Worcestershire sauce,** ½ teaspoon **salt,** ½ teaspoon **paprika,** and dash bottled **hot pepper sauce;** beat till smooth. Add 1 clove **garlic,** halved; transfer to a jar. Cover; store in the refrigerator. Remove garlic before using. Makes 1⅓ cups dressing. Use remaining dressing to top salads or to marinate chicken.

Hot Chicken-Potato Salad

Cook 8 medium **potatoes,** covered, in boiling **salted water** to cover until tender, about 30 minutes. Cool, peel, and cube. *Or,* drain four 16-ounce cans **sliced potatoes;** set aside.

In large Dutch oven cook 6 slices **bacon** till crisp. Drain and crumble bacon; reserve drippings. Cook 1 cup chopped **onion** in drippings till tender but not brown. Stir in two 10¾-ounce cans condensed **cream of celery soup;** ¾ cup **vinegar;** ¼ cup sweet **pickle relish;** one 4-ounce can **pimiento,** chopped; 2 tablespoons **sugar;** 1½ teaspoons **celery seed;** and ½ teaspoon **salt.** Bring just to boil. Stir in potatoes and 3 cups cubed cooked **chicken** *or* **turkey.** Cover; heat through. Transfer to large bowl; sprinkle with bacon. Makes 12 servings.

Cheesy Chicken-Corn Chowder

1 whole small chicken breast,
   halved lengthwise (8 ounces)
½ cup water
¼ cup chopped onion
¼ cup chopped celery
1 10¾-ounce can condensed cream
   of chicken soup
1 8¾-ounce can whole kernel
   corn
½ cup milk
½ cup shredded sharp American
   cheese (2 ounces)
2 tablespoons chopped pimiento

In medium saucepan combine chicken, water, onion, and celery. Bring to boiling. Reduce heat; cover and simmer till tender, 15 to 20 minutes. Remove chicken; cool slightly. Discard skin and bones; cut up meat. Return chicken to broth; stir in soup, undrained corn, milk, cheese, and pimiento. Cook, uncovered, till heated through, about 10 minutes, stirring occasionally. Makes 4 or 5 servings.

Microwave: *In 1½-quart glass casserole combine chicken, water, onion, and celery. Cook, covered, in countertop microwave oven till chicken and vegetables are tender, about 7 minutes. Remove chicken; cool slightly. Discard skin and bones; cut up meat. Return chicken to broth; stir in soup, undrained corn, milk, cheese, and pimiento. Micro-cook, uncovered, till heated,8 to 9 minutes; stir often.*

Cream of Chicken Soup

¼ cup butter *or* margarine
⅓ cup all-purpose flour
2 10¾-ounce cans condensed
   chicken broth
2 cups milk
1 cup finely chopped cooked
   chicken *or* turkey
   Dash pepper

In 3-quart saucepan melt butter; blend in flour. Add undiluted broth and milk. Cook and stir till slightly thickened and bubbly. Cook and stir 2 minutes longer. Stir in chicken and pepper; heat through. Serve immediately. If desired, garnish with snipped chives, parsley, or toasted slivered almonds. Makes 4 or 5 servings.

Turkey Chowder

>   2 medium potatoes, peeled
>   and cubed (2 cups)
>   1 10-ounce package frozen baby
>   lima beans
>   ½ cup chopped onion
>   ½ cup sliced celery
>   1 10¾-ounce can condensed cream
>   of chicken soup
>   1 16-ounce can tomatoes, cut up
>   1½ cups chopped cooked turkey
>   *or* chicken
>   ½ teaspoon poultry seasoning
>   ¼ teaspoon garlic salt
>   ⅛ teaspoon pepper
>   ½ cup shredded Cheddar cheese

In 3-quart saucepan combine potatoes, beans, onion, celery, and ¼ teaspoon salt. Blend 2 cups water into canned soup; add to vegetables. Cook, covered, till vegetables are tender, 35 to 45 minutes. Add undrained tomatoes, turkey, poultry seasoning, garlic salt, and pepper. Simmer 15 minutes. Sprinkle *1 tablespoon* cheese over each serving. Makes 8 servings.

Crockery Cooker: Use above ingredients plus 2 teaspoons instant chicken bouillon granules. In an electric slow crockery cooker combine potatoes, lima beans, onion, celery, ¼ teaspoon salt, and the 2 teaspoons chicken bouillon granules. Stir in soup, undrained tomatoes, turkey, poultry seasoning, garlic salt, pepper, and 2 cups water. Cover and cook on low-heat setting for 8 to 10 hours or on high-heat setting for 3½ to 4 hours. Season to taste. Stir well before serving; serve as above.

Easy Bean Chowder

>   2 tablespoons chopped onion
>   1 tablespoon butter *or* margarine
>   1 11½-ounce can condensed bean
>   with bacon soup
>   1 10¾-ounce can condensed
>   minestrone soup
>   2⅔ cups milk (2 soup cans)
>   2 cups chopped cooked chicken
>   *or* turkey

In saucepan cook onion in butter till tender but not brown. Blend in soups; stir in milk. Add chicken; heat through. Makes 6 servings.

Brunswick Stew

In large kettle or Dutch oven simmer one cut-up 6-pound stewing **chicken** in 6 cups **water** till tender, 1½ to 2 hours. Remove chicken from broth; cool. Remove meat from bones. Cube meat; discard skin and bones. Skim fat from broth. Add cubed chicken to broth. Add one 28-ounce can **tomatoes;** two 17-ounce cans whole kernel **corn,** drained; 2 cups **fresh okra,** sliced *or* one 10-ounce package **frozen cut okra;** one 10-ounce package frozen **lima beans;** 3 medium **potatoes,** peeled and cubed (3 cups); 2 large **onions,** sliced; 4 teaspoons **salt;** 1 tablespoon **sugar;** and ¼ teaspoon **pepper.** Cover and simmer till vegetables are tender and flavors are blended, about 30 minutes. Makes 16 servings.

Western-Style Turkey Soup

>   8 cups cold water
>   ½ pound dry garbanzo beans (1 cup)
>   2 1½- to 2-pound turkey legs
>   2 small onions, chopped (¾ cup)
>   2 teaspoons instant chicken
>   bouillon granules
>   1½ teaspoons dried oregano, crushed
>   1 teaspoon salt
>   1 bay leaf
>   ¼ teaspoon pepper
>   ⅓ cup regular rice
>   3 tablespoons chopped, seeded
>   canned green chili peppers
>   Snipped parsley
>   Cubed Monterey Jack cheese

Place cold water and beans in large kettle or Dutch oven. Bring to boiling; simmer 2 minutes. Remove from heat. Cover; let stand 1 hour. (*Or,* add water to beans; soak overnight.) Add turkey legs, onions, bouillon granules, oregano, salt, bay leaf, and pepper. Cover; bring to boiling. Reduce heat; simmer over low heat till beans and turkey are tender, about 1¼ hours. Add rice and chili peppers. Continue to simmer, covered, till rice is done, about 15 minutes. Discard bay leaf. Remove turkey; let cool. Remove turkey meat from bones; cube meat. Discard skin and bones. Return turkey to broth. Heat through. Season; garnish with parsley. Serve with cheese. Serves 8.

Use up that leftover Thanksgiving turkey in *Turkey Frame Soup*. This delicious family-style favorite is enriched with homemade *Old-Fashioned Egg Noodles* and dried herbs, plus plenty of fresh vegetables such as tomatoes, celery, carrots, mushrooms, cauliflower, rutabaga, and broccoli.

Soup and Spinach Dumplings

1 2½- to 3-pound broiler-fryer
    chicken, cut up
6 cups water
2 sprigs parsley
2 stalks celery, cut up
1 carrot, sliced
1 small onion, cut up
2 teaspoons salt
¼ teaspoon pepper
1 bay leaf
    Spinach Dumplings
    Snipped parsley

In large kettle or Dutch oven combine chicken and water. Add parsley sprigs, celery, carrot, onion, salt, pepper, and bay leaf. Cover and simmer till chicken is tender, about 1 hour. Remove chicken from broth. Strain broth; discard vegetables. Skim off excess fat. Return broth to pan. Remove chicken meat from bones. Chop chicken; add to broth. Set broth aside. Prepare Spinach Dumplings. Bring broth to simmering; drop in dumplings. Cook, covered, for 10 minutes. Season soup to taste with salt and pepper. Top individual servings with snipped parsley. Makes 6 servings.

Spinach Dumplings: Beat 1 **egg** with 1 tablespoon **water.** Add ⅔ cup all-purpose **flour** and ¼ teaspoon **salt.** Knead on floured surface a few minutes. Cover; let rest 20 minutes.

For filling, combine ¼ cup finely chopped **cooked spinach;** 1 **egg;** 2 tablespoons grated **Parmesan cheese;** 2 tablespoons fine dry **bread crumbs;** ⅛ teaspoon **salt;** ⅛ teaspoon dried **thyme,** crushed; and dash ground **nutmeg.** Mix ingredients thoroughly.

Roll dumpling dough ⅛ inch thick. Cut into sixteen 2-inch circles. Place 1½ teaspoons filling on half of each circle. Moisten edges with water and fold dough over. Seal edges of dough by pressing with tines of fork.

Turkey Frame Soup

Place 1 meaty **turkey frame** in large Dutch oven with 5 quarts **water;** 1 **onion,** quartered; and 4 teaspoons **salt.** Cook, covered, 1½ hours. Remove frame; cool till it can be handled. Remove meat from bones; discard bones. Remove onion from broth. Add turkey meat; 3 **tomatoes,** quartered; 1 teaspoon dried **thyme,** crushed; and ½ teaspoon dried **oregano,** crushed, to broth. Stir in 8 cups of **fresh vegetables** (any combination of uncooked sliced celery, sliced carrot, chopped onion, chopped rutabaga, sliced mushrooms, chopped broccoli, and cauliflowerets). Bring to boiling; cover and simmer for 45 minutes. Add 3 cups uncooked **Old-Fashioned Egg Noodles;** boil 15 minutes more. Makes 12 servings.

Old-Fashioned Egg Noodles

Combine 1 beaten **egg,** 2 tablespoons **milk,** and ½ teaspoon **salt.** Add enough all-purpose **flour** to make a stiff dough (about 1 cup). Roll very thin on a floured surface. Let stand 20 minutes. Roll up loosely. Slice ¼ inch wide. Unroll; spread out. Let dry for 2 hours. Store in covered container till needed. Use in recipes as directed or cook, uncovered, in boiling salted water till tender, about 10 minutes. Makes 3 cups cooked or uncooked noodles.

Turkey Soup Oriental

   2 10½-ounce cans cut asparagus
   3 cups chicken broth
   1 3-ounce can sliced mushrooms
   ½ cup coarsely chopped onion
   2 tablespoons cornstarch
  1½ cups chopped cooked turkey
  1½ cups shredded lettuce

Drain asparagus; reserve liquid. Combine asparagus liquid, broth, mushrooms, and onion. Cover; simmer till onion is tender, about 7 minutes. Blend 2 tablespoons cold water into cornstarch. Stir into broth mixture. Cook and stir till bubbly. Stir in turkey, asparagus, and dash pepper; heat through. Place some lettuce in each soup bowl; pour soup over. Top with crumbled cooked bacon, if desired. Serves 6.

Homemade Corn and Chicken Soup

   1 5- to 6-pound stewing chicken,
      cut up
  ⅓ cup chopped onion
   1 bay leaf
   6 medium ears corn or one
      16-ounce can cream-style corn
 1½ cups uncooked Old-Fashioned
      Egg Noodles
   1 cup chopped celery
   2 tablespoons snipped parsley

In kettle mix chicken, onion, bay leaf, 6 cups water, 2 teaspoons salt, and ¼ teaspoon pepper. Bring to boiling. Simmer, covered, 2 hours.

  With sharp knife, make cuts through center of corn kernels in each row of ears. Cut corn off cobs; scrape cobs. (Should equal 2 cups corn.) Remove chicken from broth; cool. Remove meat from bones. Cube meat; set aside. Skim fat from broth. Discard bay leaf. Bring broth to boiling. Add corn, noodles, celery, and parsley. Simmer, covered, till corn and noodles are barely tender, about 8 minutes. Add meat; heat through. Season to taste. Makes 8 servings.

Mulligatawny

   4 cups chicken broth
   2 cups chopped cooked chicken
   1 16-ounce can tomatoes, cut up
   1 tart apple, peeled and chopped
  ¼ cup finely chopped onion
  ¼ cup chopped carrot
  ¼ cup chopped celery
  ¼ cup chopped green pepper
   1 tablespoon snipped parsley
   2 teaspoons lemon juice
   1 teaspoon sugar
   1 teaspoon curry powder
   2 whole cloves
  ¾ teaspoon salt
   Dash pepper

In a 3-quart saucepan combine all ingredients and bring to boiling. Reduce heat; simmer, covered, for 20 minutes, stirring occasionally. Remove cloves. Makes 6 to 8 servings.

Crockery Cooker: Mix all ingredients in an electric slow crockery cooker. Cover; cook on low-heat setting for 8 to 10 hours or high-heat setting for 4 to 5 hours. Remove cloves.

Chicken-Ham Stack-Ups

    8 slices boiled ham (6 ounces)
    1 tablespoon butter *or* margarine
    2 tablespoons all-purpose flour
    ¾ cup milk
    1 cup chopped cooked chicken
    1 2-ounce can chopped mushrooms,
        drained
    2 tablespoons snipped parsley
    2 tablespoons dry sherry
    4 English muffins, split and
        toasted

Place ham in a skillet; add 2 tablespoons water. Simmer, covered, till ham is heated through, 3 to 5 minutes. (*Or,* heat ham in a 350° oven till warm.) In saucepan melt butter; blend in flour. Add milk; cook and stir till thickened and bubbly. Stir in chicken, mushrooms, parsley, and sherry. Cook and stir till heated through. On each plate place 2 muffin halves. Arrange 2 rolled ham slices atop. Spoon chicken mixture over all. Makes 4 servings.

Microwave: Wrap ham slices in waxed paper. Place ham to one side in a countertop microwave oven. At the same time, in a 2-cup glass measure micro-melt butter about 45 seconds. Blend in flour; add milk. Mix thoroughly. Micro-cook, uncovered, till thickened and bubbly, about 2½ minutes, stirring every 30 seconds. Stir in chicken, mushrooms, and parsley. Micro-cook, covered, till heated through, about 1½ minutes. Stir in sherry. Remove ham from oven. Assemble sandwiches as above.

Buying Chicken for Cooked Meat in Recipes

Here are some handy buying rules-of-thumb to figure how much raw chicken to buy for a given amount of cooked chicken. Two whole chicken breasts (10 ounces each) give about 2 cups cubed or chopped cooked chicken. A 2½- to 3-pound broiler-fryer chicken yields about 2½ cups chopped cooked meat and a 3½-pound roasting chicken provides 3 cups.

Oriental Salad Loaf

    2 cups chopped cooked chicken *or*
        turkey
    1 5-ounce can bamboo shoots,
        drained
    ½ cup sliced celery
    ½ cup mayonnaise
    1 hard-cooked egg, chopped
    2 tablespoons chopped green
        onion with tops
    2 tablespoons frozen orange juice
        concentrate
    ½ teaspoon salt
    1 loaf French bread
        Butter *or* margarine, softened
        Bibb lettuce

Combine chicken, bamboo shoots, celery, mayonnaise, chopped egg, green onion, orange juice concentrate, and salt. Chill. Cut bread in half lengthwise; wrap top half and store for another use. Scoop out center of loaf. Spread bread with butter. Arrange lettuce on bread; top with chicken salad mixture. Garnish with green pepper slices, if desired. Serves 6.

Barbecue Chicken Sandwiches

    ½ cup chopped onion
    ½ cup chopped celery
    1 clove garlic, minced
    2 tablespoons butter *or* margarine
    1 cup chili sauce
    ½ cup water
    2 tablespoons brown sugar
    2 tablespoons vinegar
    1 teaspoon Worcestershire sauce
    ¾ teaspoon chili powder
    ¼ teaspoon salt
        Dash pepper
    1½ cups shredded *or* finely cut up
        cooked chicken
    6 hamburger buns, split and
        toasted

In medium skillet cook onion, celery, and garlic in butter till tender but not brown. Stir in chili sauce, water, brown sugar, vinegar, Worcestershire, chili powder, salt, and pepper. Simmer, covered, 10 to 15 minutes, stirring occasionally. Add chicken; heat through. Serve mixture on toasted buns. Makes 6 sandwiches.

Curried Turkey Open-Facers

    1 large apple, cored
      Lemon juice
   12 thin slices cooked turkey *or*
      chicken
    2 tablespoons turkey broth *or*
      water
    ½ of a 10¾-ounce can condensed
      cream of chicken soup (⅔ cup)
    ¼ cup dairy sour cream
    3 tablespoons milk
    2 teaspoons curry powder
    6 slices French bread, toasted

Cut apple into 18 wedges; brush with lemon juice. Heat turkey in broth, covered, 4 to 5 minutes. Turn slices once. Combine soup, sour cream, milk, and curry; heat through. Place 2 turkey slices and 3 apple wedges atop each bread slice; spoon sauce over. Makes 6.

Chicken-Asparagus Stacks

    6 tablespoons butter *or* margarine
    2 tablespoons all-purpose flour
    2 packages hollandaise sauce mix
    1 teaspoon prepared mustard
 1¾ cups milk
    2 cups chopped cooked chicken *or*
      turkey
    1 10-ounce package frozen
      asparagus spears
    8 rusks

In saucepan melt butter; blend in flour, dry sauce mixes, mustard, and dash pepper. Stir in milk. Cook and stir till thickened and bubbly. Add chicken; heat through. Cook asparagus according to package directions; drain. To serve, top *four* rusks with *half* the chicken mixture. Top with remaining rusks, asparagus, and remaining chicken. Makes 4 sandwiches.

For a warm luncheon sandwich in a hurry, serve *Curried Turkey Open-Facers.* These hearty sandwiches feature toasted French bread slices topped with cooked turkey or chicken, apple wedges, and a creamy curry and sour cream sauce. To dress up the meal, add carrot curls and celery leaves.

Roast Poultry

Reach back into your childhood and rekindle memories of a holiday turkey dinner. Plump and juicy, the golden roast bird arrives at the table, and as the carving begins, slice after slice glides onto the platter. Next to the bird, bowls of sage stuffing, cranberry sauce, and rich gravy tempt already-sharpened appetites. These sights and aromas bring back the pleasing memories the traditional turkey dinner has given so often.

From simple-to-follow instructions on storing, preparing, and carving roast poultry to the many recipes for stuffings, glazes, sauces, and gravies, this chapter will help you re-create the same pleasant memories or add new ones in as many variations as your imagination desires.

Whether or not you see the family for the holidays, a festive turkey dinner with all the trimmings is one tradition you'll want to observe. This magnificent roast bird with *Bread and Butter Stuffing* well deserves to be the center of attention (see recipe, page 60).

Roasting Birds

Ham- and Rice-Stuffed Chicken

See this attractive bird on the cover—

    ¼ cup chopped onion
    1 tablespoon butter *or* margarine
    1½ cups chicken broth
    ½ cup regular rice
    ¼ teaspoon salt
      Dash pepper
    ½ cup finely chopped fully
        cooked ham
    ¼ cup dairy sour cream
    2 tablespoons snipped parsley
    1 3-pound whole broiler-fryer chicken
      Cooking oil

In saucepan cook onion in butter till tender. Add broth, uncooked rice, salt, and pepper. Bring to boiling. Reduce heat; cover and cook over low heat till liquid is absorbed, 20 to 25 minutes. Stir in ham, sour cream, and parsley. Spoon some of the stuffing into neck cavity of chicken. Skewer neck skin to back. Spoon remaining stuffing into body cavity. Tie legs securely to the tail and twist the wing tips under back of chicken.

Place bird, breast up, on rack in shallow roasting pan. Brush skin with oil. Roast in uncovered pan at 375° till done, about 1½ hours, basting occasionally with pan drippings. Garnish with lemon wedges, crab apples, and parsley sprigs, if desired. Serves 3 or 4.

Pollo Arrosto with Tarragon

In Italian, "pollo arrosto" means roast chicken—

Brush one 2½- to 3-pound whole broiler-fryer **chicken** inside and out with 2 tablespoons **lemon juice**; sprinkle with ½ teaspoon **salt**. Skewer neck skin to back; tie legs to tail. Twist wing tips under back. Combine 2 tablespoons melted **butter** and 1½ teaspoons dried **tarragon**, crushed; brush over chicken. Place, breast up, on rack in shallow roasting pan. Roast in uncovered pan at 375° till done, 1¼ to 1½ hours; baste occasionally with pan drippings. Makes 3 or 4 servings.

Cranberry-Stuffed Cornish Hens

    ⅔ cup chopped cranberries
    2 tablespoons sugar
    1 teaspoon shredded orange peel
    ½ teaspoon salt
    ⅛ teaspoon ground cinnamon
    3 cups toasted raisin bread
        cubes
    2 tablespoons butter *or*
        margarine, melted
    4 teaspoons orange juice
              • • •
    4 1- to 1½-pound Cornish
        game hens
      Salt
      Cooking oil
    ¼ cup orange juice
    2 tablespoons butter *or*
        margarine, melted

In bowl combine chopped cranberries, sugar, orange peel, ½ teaspoon salt, and cinnamon. Add raisin bread cubes; sprinkle with 2 tablespoons melted butter or margarine and the 4 teaspoons orange juice. Toss lightly to mix.

Season cavities of hens with salt. Lightly stuff birds with cranberry mixture. Pull neck skin to back of each bird and fasten securely with a small skewer. Tie legs to tail; twist wing tips under back. Place Cornish hens, breast side up, on a rack in shallow roasting pan. Brush with cooking oil; cover loosely with foil. Roast at 375° for 30 minutes.

Combine ¼ cup orange juice and 2 tablespoons melted butter or margarine. Uncover birds; baste with orange juice-butter mixture. Roast, uncovered, till done (drumstick can be twisted easily), about 1 hour longer, basting once or twice with orange juice-butter mixture. Makes 4 servings.

When a special occasion calls for just the right ▶ entrée, serve *Cranberry-Stuffed Cornish Hens*. Garnish the birds with parsley, cranberry-centered kumquat roses, and a lemon twist.

Chicken with Curry Stuffing

  ½ cup chopped onion
  ½ cup chopped celery
  ¼ cup butter *or* margarine
  1 teaspoon curry powder
  ½ teaspoon salt
  ⅛ teaspoon pepper
  5 cups dry bread cubes
  1 cup chicken broth
  1 4- to 5-pound whole roasting
      chicken
      Cooking oil

In saucepan cook onion and celery in butter till tender but not brown. Stir in curry powder, salt, and pepper. Combine with bread cubes; toss with enough chicken broth to moisten.

Rub neck and body cavities of chicken with salt; stuff loosely with bread mixture. Skewer neck skin to back. Tie legs securely to tail. Twist wing tips under back.

Place chicken, breast side up, on a rack in shallow roasting pan. Brush skin with cooking oil. Roast in uncovered pan at 375° till done, 2 to 2½ hours. Baste occasionally with pan drippings. Makes 4 servings.

Microwave: In 2-quart glass bowl combine onion, celery, and butter. Cook, covered, in countertop microwave oven till vegetables are tender, about 2½ minutes. Add curry powder, salt, and pepper. Stir in bread cubes; toss with enough chicken broth to moisten.

*Prepare chicken for roasting as above, using wooden picks for skewers. Place chicken, breast side **down**, on non-metal rack (or use inverted saucers) in 12x7½x2-inch glass baking dish. Allow 7 minutes per pound for total cooking time. Micro-cook for half the cooking time, turning dish once. Turn chicken breast up. Micro-cook for remaining time, turning dish once. Baste with pan drippings or brush with oil each time dish or chicken is turned. If your oven manufacturer allows, cover wing tips and ends of legs with small pieces of foil to prevent over-browning.*

*Chicken is done when meat thermometer registers 180°. Insert thermometer after chicken is removed from microwave oven. **Do not use** while oven is operating. Before carving, cover chicken with foil; let stand 10 minutes (temperature should rise to 185°). Arrange sliced meat on a warm serving platter. Pass stuffing.*

Chicken and Wine-Cream Sauce

Skewer neck skin to back of one 2½- to 3-pound whole broiler-fryer **chicken.** Tie legs to tail; twist wings under back. Place, breast up, on rack in shallow roasting pan. Season; brush with **cooking oil.** Roast in uncovered pan at 375° for 1¼ to 1½ hours; baste with drippings. Remove; keep warm. Skim fat from drippings. Pour drippings into saucepan; add 2 cups fresh **mushrooms,** sliced, and ⅓ cup dry **white wine.** Cook, covered, 7 minutes. Blend ½ cup **whipping cream** into 1 tablespoon **cornstarch;** stir into wine. Cook and stir till bubbly. Season. Stir in 1 tablespoon **brandy.** Pass sauce with chicken. Makes 3 or 4 servings.

Microwave-Thawed Poultry

Thaw poultry quickly using *defrost setting* of countertop microwave oven. Leave bird in original plastic wrapping, but remove metal clip. Place in shallow glass baking dish. If your oven manufacturer allows, place small pieces of foil over breast, wing tips, or ends of legs if they begin cooking before bird thaws.

Chicken: Broiler-fryer (2½- to 3-pound)—For *cut-up,* micro-thaw 18 to 20 minutes; separate after 12 minutes. For *whole,* micro-thaw, breast up, 10 minutes. Invert; micro-thaw 5 to 10 minutes. Let either stand 5 minutes.

Roasting chicken (4- to 5-pound)—Micro-thaw *whole* bird, breast up, 10 minutes; let stand 10 minutes. Micro-thaw, breast down, for 10 minutes; let stand 10 minutes. Micro-thaw, breast up, 5 to 10 minutes longer.

Cornish Game Hen: Micro-thaw one 1- to 1½-pound hen 12 to 15 minutes, 2 hens 16 to 20 minutes, or 4 hens 25 to 30 minutes. Micro-thaw, breast down, half the time. Invert; micro-thaw, breast up, remaining time. Let stand in cool water for 10 minutes.

Turkey: Micro-thaw one 7- to 8-pound *whole* turkey, breast up, 15 minutes; let stand 5 minutes; give bird quarter turn. Repeat micro-thawing, standing, and turning for total of 45 to 50 minutes. Let stand 30 minutes.

Boneless Turkey Roast: Remove one 3-pound roast from foil. Micro-thaw 15 minutes; invert. Micro-thaw 15 minutes more. Let stand 10 minutes before using.

Wine-Basted Capons

½ cup dried currants
  Boiling water
10 cups French bread cubes
1¼ cups coarsely crumbled soda
    crackers (about 20 crackers)
¼ teaspoon ground nutmeg
¼ teaspoon ground allspice
⅛ teaspoon pepper
½ cup chopped onion
½ cup chopped celery
½ cup butter *or* margarine
1 10¾-ounce can condensed
    cream of chicken soup
2 beaten eggs
½ cup rosé wine
2 5- to 6-pound whole capons *or*
    roasting chickens
½ cup rosé wine
1 tablespoon lemon juice
¼ cup all-purpose flour

Cover currants with boiling water. Let stand for 10 minutes. Drain well. Combine bread cubes, cracker crumbs, nutmeg, allspice, and pepper. In medium saucepan cook onion and celery in butter till tender but not brown; add soup, eggs, ½ cup wine, and drained currants. Pour over bread mixture; toss to mix.

Lightly spoon stuffing into body cavities of birds. (Bake any additional stuffing in small covered casserole last half hour of roasting.) Tuck legs under band of skin or tie securely to tail. Twist wing tips under back. Place birds, breast side up, on rack in shallow roasting pan. Roast in uncovered pan at 375° for 1½ hours. Combine ½ cup wine and lemon juice; pour over birds. Continue roasting till done, 1 to 1¼ hours, basting often with liquid in pan. Remove birds to platter; keep warm.

Leaving crusty bits in pan, pour pan juices into a large measuring cup. Skim off fat, reserving 3 to 4 tablespoons. Return reserved fat to pan. Stir in flour; blend well. Cook and stir over low heat till bubbly. Remove pan from heat. Add water to juices in measuring cup to make 2 cups liquid; add to flour mixture all at once. Return to heat; cook and stir till thickened and bubbly. Season to taste. Serve with roast birds. Serves 10 to 12.

Helpful Storing and Thawing Guides

Storing Fresh Poultry: Rinse poultry; pat dry; separate into desired portions. Remove giblets. *To refrigerate,* wrap poultry loosely in waxed paper or clear plastic wrap. Wrap giblets loosely; store separately; cook promptly. *To freeze,* wrap poultry tightly in moisture-vaporproof material. Wrap and freeze giblets separately. Do not freeze stuffed poultry.
Storing Cooked Poultry: Remove stuffing and meat from bones of cooked poultry as soon as possible. Cool; *refrigerate* promptly. Store meat, stuffing, and gravy separately. *To freeze cooked poultry,* cool quickly. Divide into meal-size portions. Wrap tightly in moisture-vaporproof material; seal, label, and freeze. Never freeze stuffed poultry. Do not refreeze poultry that has been thawed.
Thawing Frozen Poultry: Thaw most poultry before cooking. (For exceptions, see tip on page 34.) Thaw in refrigerator in original wrap. For large whole birds, follow thawing directions on label, or thaw in refrigerator in original wrap 2 to 3 days. For faster defrosting, place frozen bird (in original wrap or in a plastic bag) in *cold* water. Allow 30 to 60 minutes thawing time for small chickens and up to 6 to 8 hours for large turkeys. Change the water frequently.

Storage Time

Poultry	Refrig.	Freezer
Ready-to-cook:		
Chicken, whole	1-2 days	12 months
Chicken, cut up	1-2 days	6 months
Turkey, whole (thawed)	1-2 days	6 months
Cooked:		
Poultry with liquid	1-2 days	6 months
Poultry without liquid	1-2 days	1 month
Gravy and stuffing	1-2 days	2 months

Fruit-Stuffed Cornish Hens

   2 medium oranges
   ¼ cup chopped onion
   2 tablespoons slivered almonds
   2 tablespoons butter *or* margarine
   4 cups dry bread cubes
   ¼ cup light raisins
   ½ teaspoon salt
   6 1- to 1½-pound Cornish
      game hens
      Cooking oil
   ½ cup Burgundy
   ¼ cup butter *or* margarine, melted
   2 tablespoons orange juice

Peel and cut up oranges over bowl to catch juice. Cook onion and almonds in 2 tablespoons butter for 5 minutes. Toss with chopped oranges and juice, bread cubes, raisins, and salt. Season hens with salt and pepper. Lightly stuff birds with bread mixture. Skewer neck skin to back; tie legs to tail; twist wing tips under back. Place hens, breast side up, on rack in shallow roasting pan. Brush with oil; cover loosely with foil. Roast at 375° for 30 minutes.

Meanwhile, combine wine, melted butter, and orange juice. Uncover hens; baste with wine mixture. Roast, uncovered, till done, 1 to 1¼ hours longer, basting frequently with wine mixture. Makes 6 servings.

Turkey Wellington

Roast one 2- to 3-pound frozen boneless **turkey roast** according to package directions till meat thermometer inserted in center reaches 160°. Remove skin and cord; place roast in shallow pan. Spoon ½ cup **cranberry-orange relish** over roast. Continue roasting, uncovered, till meat thermometer registers 170°.

Meanwhile, on floured surface separate dough from 1 package refrigerated **crescent rolls** (8 rolls) into 4 rectangles. Overlap to form one large rectangle; press perforations and seams to seal. Roll to 15x10-inch rectangle.

Remove roast from oven. Turn oven temperature to 375°. Place dough over turkey, molding to shape of roast. Trim excess dough; use for cutouts to decorate top of roast. Brush dough with 1 beaten **egg**. Bake, uncovered, till browned, 10 to 15 minutes. Serves 8 to 10.

Roast Sweet-Sour Chickens

Drain one 8¼-ounce can crushed **pineapple,** reserving 1 tablespoon syrup. Combine pineapple, 4 cups dry **bread cubes,** ½ cup flaked **coconut,** ½ cup chopped **celery,** ½ teaspoon **salt,** and ¼ teaspoon **poultry seasoning.** Drizzle with ¼ cup melted **butter;** toss lightly. For moist stuffing, add the reserved syrup.

Rub neck and body cavities of two 2½- to 3-pound whole broiler-fryer **chickens** with **salt.** Stuff loosely with bread mixture. Skewer neck skin to back. Tie legs to tail; twist wing tips under back. Place chickens, breast up, on rack in shallow roasting pan. Rub skin with **cooking oil.** Roast in uncovered pan at 375° till done, 1¼ to 1½ hours, brushing with pan drippings. Remove to platter; keep warm.

Skim off fat from pan drippings. Measure drippings; add **water** to make 1½ cups liquid. In small saucepan blend 2 tablespoons **cornstarch,** 2 tablespoons **brown sugar,** and ¼ teaspoon **salt.** Add drippings. Cook and stir till bubbly. Stir in 1 tablespoon **lemon juice.** Pass sauce with chickens. Makes 6 to 8 servings.

Apricot-Sauced Duckling

   1 small orange
   1 4- to 5-pound domestic duckling
   1 medium onion, cut in wedges
   1 small apple, halved and cored
   1 12-ounce can apricot nectar
   2 teaspoons instant chicken
      bouillon granules
   1 tablespoon cornstarch

Peel orange; scrape white membrane from peel. Cut outer portion of peel into thin strips; set aside. Quarter orange. Lightly salt cavity of duckling. Stuff loosely with orange, onion, and apple. Skewer neck skin to back; tie legs to tail; twist wings under back. Prick skin all over with fork. Place, breast up, on rack in shallow roasting pan. Roast in uncovered pan at 375° for 1¾ to 2 hours; spoon off fat.

Meanwhile, stir nectar, bouillon granules, and reserved peel into cornstarch in saucepan. Cook and stir till bubbly. Brush duckling with a little sauce; roast till done, about 15 minutes longer. Discard stuffing, if desired. Pass remaining sauce. Makes 3 or 4 servings.

It's a royal feast when you serve *Glazed Duckling* with braised celery and preserved kumquats. To obtain the regal, golden-brown dish, baste the roast duckling with honey and soy sauce.

Glazed Duckling

> 1 4- to 5-pound domestic duckling
> 1 teaspoon salt
>   Celery tops
> 1 medium onion, quartered
> ¼ cup honey
> 1 tablespoon soy sauce
> 1 tablespoon all-purpose flour

Season duckling with the salt; stuff body cavity with celery tops and quartered onion. Skewer neck skin to back; tie legs to tail. Twist wing tips under back. Prick skin all over with fork to allow fat to escape.

Place duckling, breast up, on rack in shallow roasting pan. Roast in uncovered pan at 375° for 1¾ to 2 hours, spooning off excess fat. Add ¾ cup water to roasting pan. Combine honey and soy sauce; baste duckling. Roast till drumstick moves easily in socket, about 15 minutes longer, basting occasionally with honey-soy mixture. Discard stuffing, if desired. Remove duckling to platter; keep warm.

Blend ½ cup cold water into flour; stir into pan juices. Cook, stirring constantly, till thickened and bubbly. Season to taste with salt and pepper. Serve sauce with duckling. Garnish duckling with preserved kumquats and celery tops, if desired. Makes 3 or 4 servings.

To roast in electric skillet: Prepare duckling for roasting as directed. Place, breast up, on rack in electric skillet. Cover and cook at 325° setting for 2 hours. Unplug skillet; *let cool 5 minutes.* Then, remove cover *carefully.* Pour off fat. Add 1¼ cups water to skillet. Mix honey and soy sauce; baste duckling. Cover and continue cooking at 275° till done, about 30 minutes more. Discard stuffing, if desired. Remove duckling to platter; keep warm. Blend ½ cup cold water into flour; stir into skillet. Cook and stir till thickened and bubbly. Season to taste. Serve as above.

Roasting Chart for Domestic Birds

Preparation for Roasting: Rinse bird and pat dry with paper toweling. Rub inside of cavities with salt, if desired. Do not stuff the bird until just before cooking.

To stuff bird, spoon some of the stuffing loosely into neck cavity; pull the neck skin to the back of the bird and fasten securely with a small skewer. Lightly spoon remaining stuffing into the body cavity. If opening has a band of skin across the tail, tuck drumsticks under band; if not present, tie legs securely to tail. Twist wing tips under back.

For unstuffed bird, place quartered onions and celery in body cavity, if desired. Prepare and roast. Discard stuffing, if desired.

Roasting Directions: Place bird, breast side up, on a rack in a shallow roasting pan. Brush skin of bird, *except* duckling and goose, with cooking oil. If meat thermometer is used, insert in center of inside thigh muscle, making sure bulb does not touch bone.

Roast in uncovered pan (unless specified) according to the chart below. When bird is two-thirds done, cut band of skin or string between legs so thighs will cook evenly. Continue roasting until bird is done. Remove bird from oven; cover loosely with foil to keep warm. Let stand 15 minutes before carving.

Tests for Doneness: The meat thermometer inserted in thigh should register 185°.

Also, the thickest part of the drumstick should feel very soft when pressed between fingers protected with paper toweling. The drumstick should move up and down and twist easily in the socket.

Remember, each bird differs in size, shape, or variety. Because of these differences, roasting times can only be approximate.

Poultry	Ready-to-Cook Weight	Oven Temp.	Guide to Roasting Time	Special Instructions
Chicken	1½-2 lbs. 2½-3 lbs. 3½-4 lbs. 4½-5 lbs.	400° 375° 375° 375°	1-1¼ hrs. 1¼-1½ hrs. 1¾-2 hrs. 2¼-2½ hrs.	Brush dry areas of skin occasionally with pan drippings. Cover chicken loosely with foil.
Capon	4-7 lbs.	375°	2-3 hrs.	Brush the dry areas with pan drippings. Roast as above.
Cornish Game Hen	1-1½ lbs.	375°	1½ hrs.	Cover loosely with foil and roast for ½ hour. Uncover and roast until done, about 1 hour. If desired, baste occasionally the last hour.
Turkey	6-8 lbs. 8-12 lbs. 12-16 lbs. 16-20 lbs. 20-24 lbs.	325° 325° 325° 325° 325°	3½-4 hrs. 4-4½ hrs. 4½-5½ hrs. 5½-6½ hrs. 6½-7½ hrs.	Cover bird loosely with foil. Press lightly at the end of drumsticks and neck; leave air space between bird and foil. Baste bird occasionally, if desired. Roast, uncovered, the last 45 minutes or until turkey is done.

Roasting Chart for Domestic Birds (continued)

Poultry	Ready-to-Cook Weight	Oven Temp.	Guide to Roasting Time	Special Instructions
Foil-Wrapped Turkey	7-9 lbs. 10-13 lbs. 14-17 lbs. 18-21 lbs. 22-24 lbs.	450° 450° 450° 450° 450°	2¼-2½ hrs. 2¾-3 hrs. 3-3¼ hrs. 3¼-3½ hrs. 3¼-3¾ hrs.	Place turkey, breast up, in the center of greased, wide, heavy foil. Bring ends of foil up over breast; overlap fold and press up against ends of turkey. Place bird in shallow roasting pan (no rack). Open foil the last 20 minutes to brown the turkey.
Domestic Duckling	3-5 lbs.	375°	1½-2¼ hrs.	Prick skin well all over to allow fat to escape. During roasting, spoon off excess fat. Do not rub with oil.
Domestic Goose	7-9 lbs. 9-11 lbs. 11-13 lbs.	350° 350° 350°	2½-3 hrs. 3-3½ hrs. 3½-4 hrs.	Prick skin well all over to allow fat to escape. During roasting, spoon off excess fat. Do not rub with oil.
Guinea Hen	1½-2 lbs. 2-2½ lbs.	375° 375°	¾-1 hr. 1-1½ hrs.	Lay bacon over breast. Roast loosely covered with foil. Uncover guinea hen the last 20 minutes.

To roast turkey in a covered roasting pan:

Rinse turkey and pat dry. Stuff, if desired; prepare for roasting as directed in chart. Place turkey, breast up, on rack in roasting pan. Brush bird with cooking oil or melted butter. Insert meat thermometer in center of inside thigh muscle; make sure bulb does not touch bone. Do not add water. Cover pan with a lid or cover tightly with foil. Roast an 11- to 12-pound turkey, for example, at 350° for 3 hours. Remove cover; cut band of skin or string between legs. Baste turkey with pan drippings. Continue roasting, uncovered, till done, about 1 hour. When turkey is done, meat thermometer should register 185° and drumstick should twist easily in socket. Turkey will not be as golden as when roasted in uncovered pan.

To roast turkey in commercial cooking bag:

Rinse turkey and pat dry. Stuff, if desired; prepare for roasting as directed in chart. Place 1 tablespoon all-purpose flour in the commercial cooking bag; shake to coat interior. Place bag in large roasting pan. Brush turkey with cooking oil or melted butter. Place turkey inside bag, breast side up. Close bag loosely with twist tie. Make six ½-inch slits in top of bag to allow steam to escape. Roast according to manufacturer's directions. About 15 minutes before roasting time is up, cut the bag open. Insert meat thermometer in center of inside thigh muscle of turkey, making sure bulb does not touch bone. When done, meat thermometer should register 185° and drumstick should move up and down and twist easily in socket.

Stuffing Poultry

Spoon stuffing into neck cavity. Skewer neck skin to back. Place bird, neck end down, in a bowl. Lightly spoon stuffing into body cavity — do not pack. Shake down to fill bird.

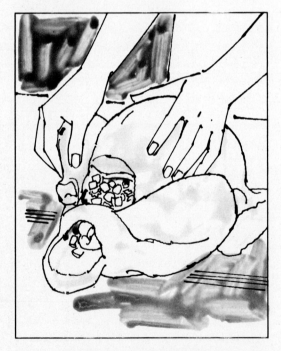

If opening of bird has a band of skin across the tail, tuck drumsticks under band. If not present, tie the legs securely to the tail.

Carving Styles

Standard Style

1. Remove bird from oven and let stand 15 minutes before carving; cover to keep warm. Place bird on carving board or on a platter protected by a board. Grasp leg with fingers; pull leg away from body. Cut through meat between thigh and body. With the tip of the knife, disjoint thighbone from backbone.

2. Holding leg vertically, large end down, slice meat parallel to bone and under some tendons, turning leg for even slices. *Or,* first separate thigh and drumstick. Slice thigh meat by cutting slices parallel to the bone.

3. Before carving white meat, make a deep horizontal cut into breast close to wing. Note that the wing tips have been twisted under the back before roasting so that carving can be done without removing wings.

4. Cut thin slices from top of breast down to horizontal cut. Final smaller slices can follow curve of breastbone. Repeat each step to carve the other side of the bird.

Side Style

1. Use this style when carving in the kitchen or when carving half a bird. Place two slices of bread under the bird to steady it. Lay bird on side, breast away from you. Remove wing between wing joint and breast.

2. Slice dark meat from inside of drumstick and thigh until thighbone is exposed. Lift drumstick and cut off between thigh and drumstick. Slice remaining meat from drumstick.

3. With knife point, cut completely around thighbone. Lift thighbone up and away from the bird; remove. Slice dark meat just above removed thighbone. If desired, cut an opening below thigh area to reach stuffing.

4. Make deep vertical cut in breast just in front of wing joint to serve as base for all breast meat slices. Start halfway up breast and slice to vertical cut. Start each new slice slightly closer to center of breast. Keep slices thin and even. Turn bird; carve other side.

How to Carve Poultry

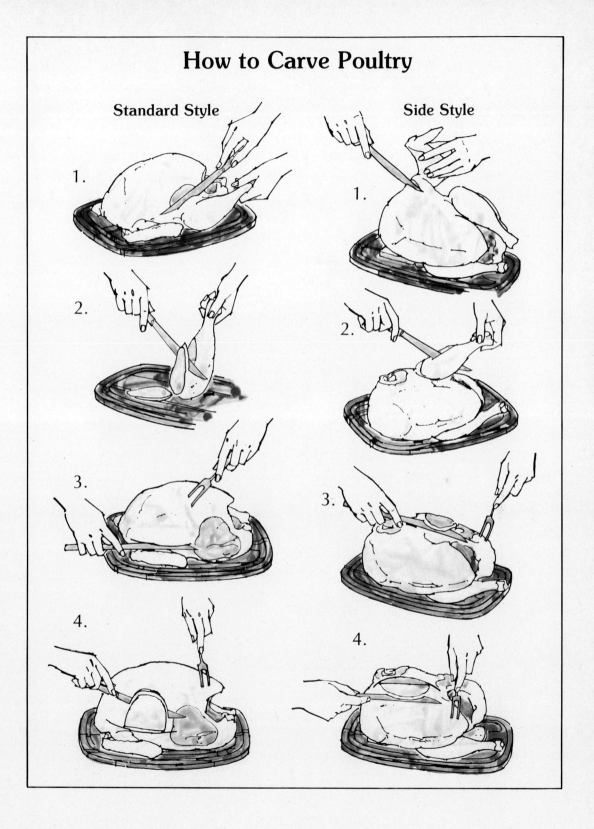

Standard Style

1.

2.

3.

4.

Side Style

1.

2.

3.

4.

Stuffings, Sauces, and Gravies

Old-Fashioned Bread Stuffing

½ cup chopped onion
½ cup butter *or* margarine
1 teaspoon poultry seasoning
    or ground sage
½ teaspoon salt
⅛ teaspoon pepper
8 cups dry bread cubes
1 cup chicken broth *or* water

Cook onion in butter till tender; add poultry seasoning or sage, salt, and pepper. Combine with bread cubes. Drizzle with broth; toss to mix well. Use to stuff a 10-pound turkey (or two 4- to 5-pound roasting chickens) *or* bake, covered, in a 2-quart casserole at 325° for 40 to 45 minutes. Makes 6 to 7 cups.

Potato Dressing

¾ cup chopped onion
¼ cup chopped celery
¼ cup butter *or* margarine
2 medium potatoes, cooked and
    mashed (2 cups)
1½ cups soft bread crumbs
2 beaten eggs
2 tablespoons snipped parsley
¾ teaspoon salt
½ teaspoon dried marjoram,
    crushed
⅛ teaspoon pepper

In skillet cook onion and celery in butter till tender but not brown. Combine with remaining ingredients; mix thoroughly. Use to stuff a 5-pound domestic duckling (or one 4- to 5-pound roasting chicken) *or* bake, covered, in a 1-quart casserole at 375° about 45 minutes. Makes about 3 cups stuffing.

◀ **Bake a fancy stuffing** outside the bird. Prepare *Bacon Stuffing Balls* in muffin pans, shape a *Corn Bread Stuffing Loaf* (see recipes, page 63), or cook *Granola-Rice Stuffing* in a favorite casserole.

Granola-Rice Stuffing

1 small orange
1½ cups cooked rice
1 cup granola cereal
1 small apple, peeled, cored, and
    chopped (⅔ cup)
¾ teaspoon salt
¼ teaspoon ground cinnamon
⅓ cup chopped celery
¼ cup chopped onion
2 tablespoons butter *or* margarine

Peel and section orange over medium-size bowl to catch juice. Chop orange sections (should have ⅓ cup); add to juice in bowl. Add cooked rice, granola cereal, chopped apple, salt, and cinnamon. Set aside.

In small saucepan cook celery and onion in butter or margarine till tender but not brown. Add to rice mixture, tossing lightly till well mixed. Use to stuff six 1- to 1½-pound Cornish game hens (or two 2½- to 3-pound broiler-fryer chickens) *or* bake, covered, in a 1-quart casserole at 375° for 25 to 30 minutes. Makes about 3½ cups stuffing.

Rice and Vegetable Stuffing

1 cup grated carrot
½ cup chopped green onion
    with tops
½ cup snipped parsley
2 tablespoons butter *or* margarine
1 cup regular rice
3 cups chicken broth
½ teaspoon salt
Dash pepper

In saucepan cook carrot, onion, and parsley in butter for 10 minutes, stirring frequently. Add uncooked rice; stir to mix well. Add broth, salt, and pepper. Cook, covered, over low heat till rice is done, about 20 minutes. Use to stuff two 3- to 4-pound roasting chickens (or one 6- to 7-pound capon) *or* bake, covered, in a 1½-quart casserole at 375° for 20 to 25 minutes. Makes about 5 cups.

Bread and Butter Stuffing

Triple recipe for large turkey shown on page 46—

> 8 slices bread
> 6 tablespoons butter *or* margarine
> ¼ cup chopped onion
> ¼ cup chopped celery
> ¾ cup chicken broth *or* water
> ½ teaspoon ground sage
> ¼ teaspoon dried thyme, crushed
> ¼ teaspoon salt
> ¼ teaspoon pepper

Toast bread; spread with butter. Cut into cubes. In covered saucepan cook onion and celery in broth about 5 minutes. Stir in seasonings. Combine with toast cubes; toss lightly. Add ¼ cup more broth for moist stuffing, if desired. Use to stuff a 5-pound roasting chicken *or* bake, covered, in greased 1-quart casserole at 375° about 30 minutes. Makes about 4 cups.

Mincemeat Stuffing

> 1 9-ounce package instant
>   condensed mincemeat
> 1 cup chopped onion
> ½ cup butter *or* margarine
> 1 tablespoon poultry seasoning
> 1 teaspoon salt
> 12 cups dry bread cubes

In saucepan combine mincemeat and 1¾ cups water. Bring to boiling; simmer till slightly thickened, 1 to 2 minutes. In skillet cook onion in butter till tender. Add poultry seasoning, salt, and the cooked mincemeat. Combine with bread cubes; toss lightly. Use to stuff one 10-pound turkey (or two 5-pound domestic ducklings) *or* bake, covered, in 2-quart casserole at 325° for 35 to 40 minutes. Makes 8 cups.

Herbed Barley Stuffing

In saucepan cook 1 cup quick-cooking **barley** and ½ cup chopped **onion** in ¼ cup **butter** till golden, stirring often. Add 2 cups **chicken broth,** two 3-ounce cans sliced **mushrooms,** 1 teaspoon **poultry seasoning,** ½ teaspoon **salt,** and dash **pepper.** Bake, covered, in 1½-quart casserole at 350° about 1 hour. Top with 2 tablespoons snipped **parsley.** Serves 6 to 8.

Grandma's Chestnut Stuffing

> 1 pound fresh chestnuts
> 1½ pounds ground beef
> ½ pound bulk pork sausage
> 1 cup chopped onion
> 1 cup chopped celery
>   • • •
> 3½ cups turkey *or* chicken
>   broth
> 1 cup regular rice
> 1 cup raisins
> ½ cup slivered almonds *or*
>   pine nuts
> 2 tablespoons turkey *or* chicken
>   drippings (optional)
> 1½ teaspoons salt
> 1 teaspoon ground cinnamon
> ¼ teaspoon pepper
> 2 beaten eggs

Cut a slash in chestnuts with a sharp knife. Roast on baking sheet at 450° for 5 to 6 minutes; cool. Peel and coarsely chop. In a 12-inch skillet cook ground beef, sausage, onion, and celery till meat is browned and vegetables are tender. Drain off fat. Add *3 cups* of the broth, chestnuts, uncooked rice, raisins, almonds, drippings, salt, cinnamon, and pepper. Cover; simmer for 30 minutes. Remove from heat. Combine remaining ½ cup broth and eggs; stir into meat-rice mixture. Use to stuff a 16- to 18-pound turkey *or* bake, covered, in two 1½-quart casseroles at 325° for 30 to 35 minutes. Makes about 9 cups.

 Try Casserole-Baked Stuffings

When baking stuffing in a casserole, add liquid to compensate for juices that ordinarily would come from the bird. Add an extra ¼ cup liquid (broth, water, or other liquid used in the recipe) when preparing the stuffing. Add more as needed, depending on the quantity of stuffing and your preference for moist or dry stuffing. Don't be afraid to baste the stuffing with additional liquid as it bakes.

Oyster-Corn Stuffing

4 cups soft bread cubes
½ of an 8-ounce package corn
    bread stuffing mix (2 cups)
2 tablespoons finely chopped
    onion
1½ teaspoons ground sage
1 teaspoon salt
  Dash pepper
1 10-ounce can frozen oysters,
    thawed
¼ cup butter *or* margarine, melted
¼ cup water

In a large mixing bowl toss together bread cubes, corn bread stuffing mix, chopped onion, sage, salt, and pepper. Drain the oysters, reserving liquid. Chop oysters; add to bread mixture with ½ cup reserved oyster liquid, melted butter, and water. Toss lightly to mix well. Use to stuff an 8-pound turkey (or two 3- to 4-pound roasting chickens) *or* bake, covered, in a 2-quart casserole at 325° about 35 minutes. Makes about 6 cups stuffing.

Wheat Bread and Apple Stuffing

1 cup chicken broth
½ cup chopped celery
¼ cup chopped onion
¼ cup butter *or* margarine
½ teaspoon salt
4 cups dry whole wheat
    bread cubes
2 medium apples, peeled, cored,
    and finely chopped
½ cup chopped pecans
1 teaspoon ground sage
¼ teaspoon ground cinnamon
⅛ teaspoon pepper

In a 1-quart saucepan combine chicken broth, celery, onion, butter, and salt. Cover and bring to boiling; simmer till vegetables are tender, about 5 minutes. In a large mixing bowl combine bread cubes, chopped apple, pecans, sage, cinnamon, and pepper. Pour broth mixture over; toss lightly to moisten. Use to stuff an 8- to 10-pound turkey (or a 9- to 11-pound domestic goose) *or* bake, covered, in a greased 1½-quart casserole at 325° about 30 minutes. Makes about 6 cups.

Chicken Liver Stuffing

½ pound chicken livers
3 tablespoons butter *or* margarine
½ cup chopped onion
½ cup chopped celery
½ cup chopped green pepper
2 beaten eggs
1 teaspoon salt
1 teaspoon Worcestershire sauce
  Dash pepper
4 cups dry bread cubes
¾ cup chicken broth *or* water

In skillet cook livers in butter over medium heat just till livers are no longer pink, about 6 minutes. Remove from skillet, reserving drippings; finely chop livers. In same skillet cook onion, celery, and green pepper in reserved drippings till tender, about 10 minutes. In mixing bowl combine eggs, salt, Worcestershire, and pepper. Stir in livers and vegetables. Add bread cubes; mix well. Toss with enough broth to moisten. Use to stuff a 6-pound capon (or two 2½- to 3-pound broiler-fryer chickens) *or* bake, covered, in a greased 1-quart casserole at 375° about 25 minutes. Makes about 4 cups.

Mushroom-Nut Stuffing

1½ cups sliced fresh mushrooms
1⅓ cups quick-cooking rice
¼ cup chopped onion
¼ cup snipped celery leaves
1½ teaspoons salt
¼ teaspoon dried oregano,
    crushed
¼ teaspoon ground sage
¼ teaspoon dried thyme, crushed
  Dash pepper
¼ cup butter *or* margarine
⅓ cup chopped pecans

In saucepan cook mushrooms, rice, onion, celery leaves, salt, oregano, sage, thyme, and pepper in butter till vegetables are tender. Stir in 1½ cups water. Simmer, uncovered, till most of water is absorbed, 6 to 8 minutes; stir once or twice. Add pecans; mix lightly. Use to stuff a 5- to 7-pound capon (or six 1- to 1½-pound Cornish game hens) *or* bake, covered, in a 1-quart casserole at 375° for 20 to 25 minutes. Makes about 4 cups.

An alternate method of carving roast turkey with *Giblet Stuffing* allows guests to easily serve themselves from a buffet table. To carve, start at the breastbone. Following the curve of the bird, cut a series of diagonal slices with an electric knife, then cut down at a right angle to loosen the slices.

Giblet Stuffing

    Turkey *or* chicken giblets
1 cup shredded carrot
1 cup chopped celery
⅓ cup chopped onion
½ cup butter *or* margarine
2 teaspoons ground sage
½ teaspoon salt
¼ teaspoon pepper
7 cups dry bread cubes

In a small saucepan cook the giblets in lightly salted water to cover till tender, about 1 hour. Drain giblets, reserving ½ cup cooking liquid. Chop the cooked giblets. In skillet cook carrot, celery, and onion in butter or margarine till tender. Add sage, salt, pepper, and chopped cooked giblets. Combine with bread cubes; toss with reserved cooking liquid to mix well. Use to stuff a 10- to 12-pound turkey (or two 5-pound roasting chickens) *or* bake, covered, in a 2-quart casserole at 325° for 40 to 45 minutes. Makes about 7 cups.

Ground Beef 'n Raisin Stuffing

4 ounces ground beef
¼ cup chopped onion
¼ cup raisins
2 tablespoons snipped parsley
1 teaspoon Worcestershire sauce
¾ teaspoon ground sage
    Dash pepper
1 beaten egg
1 cup chicken broth
5 cups coarsely crumbled corn
    bread

In medium saucepan cook beef and onion till meat is browned and onion is tender. Remove from heat; drain off excess fat. Stir in raisins, parsley, Worcestershire sauce, sage, and pepper. Blend in beaten egg and chicken broth. Combine with corn bread; toss to mix well. Use to stuff two 2½- to 3-pound broiler-fryer chickens (or one 6- to 7-pound capon) *or* bake, covered, in a 1-quart casserole at 375° about 25 minutes. Makes about 4 cups.

Sweet Potato-Apple Stuffing

1 17-ounce can sweet potatoes
   (vacuum pack)
1 medium apple, peeled, cored,
   and chopped (1 cup)
⅓ cup chopped onion
6 tablespoons butter *or* margarine
1 tablespoon sugar
1 teaspoon salt
¼ teaspoon ground nutmeg
2 cups soft bread cubes

Mash sweet potatoes. In skillet cook apple and onion in butter or margarine till tender. Stir in sugar, salt, and nutmeg. Combine with sweet potatoes and bread cubes; mix well. Use to stuff two 3-pound broiler-fryer chickens (or a 5-pound domestic duckling) *or* bake, covered, in a 1-quart casserole at 375° about 25 minutes. Makes about 4 cups.

Corn Bread Stuffing Loaf

An old favorite made into a loaf, shown on page 58—

1 cup chopped celery with leaves
½ cup chopped onion
¾ cup chicken broth
2 beaten eggs
⅓ cup mayonnaise *or* salad
   dressing
1 teaspoon poultry seasoning
½ teaspoon ground sage
¼ teaspoon salt
Chopped cooked giblets
   (optional)
6 cups coarsely crumbled corn
   bread
Celery leaves

In small saucepan cook chopped celery and onion, covered, in chicken broth till vegetables are tender, about 5 minutes. Do not drain.

In large bowl combine eggs, mayonnaise or salad dressing, poultry seasoning, sage, salt, giblets, and vegetables with broth. Add corn bread; toss lightly to mix. If desired, add ¼ cup more broth for a moist stuffing.

In a 10x6x2-inch baking dish shape mixture into a loaf. Cover with foil. Bake at 400° till heated through, 25 to 30 minutes; uncover the last 5 minutes to brown slightly. Garnish with celery leaves. Makes 8 to 10 servings.

Corn Bread Dressing

Southern Corn Bread
1 cup chopped celery with leaves
1 cup chopped onion
2 cups chicken broth
2 beaten eggs
1 teaspoon poultry seasoning
¼ teaspoon salt

Prepare Southern Corn Bread; cool. Crumble enough corn bread to make 6 cups. Cook celery and onion in broth for 5 minutes; cool. In mixing bowl combine eggs with broth mixture, poultry seasoning, salt, and crumbled corn bread. Use to stuff an 8-pound turkey (or two 4- to 5-pound domestic ducklings) *or* bake, covered, in a greased 1½-quart casserole at 325° for 30 to 35 minutes. Makes about 6 cups.

Southern Corn Bread: In mixing bowl stir together 1½ cups yellow **cornmeal,** ½ cup all-purpose **flour,** 1 teaspoon **baking soda,** and ½ teaspoon **salt.** Stir in 1½ cups **buttermilk,** 2 tablespoons melted **lard** *or* **shortening,** and 1 beaten **egg;** mix well. Pour corn bread batter into greased 9x9x2-inch baking pan. Bake at 400° about 20 minutes.

Bacon Stuffing Balls

Pictured on page 58, try these distinctive stuffing balls with creamed chicken or turkey—

6 bacon slices
1 cup chopped celery
½ cup chopped onion
2 beaten eggs
1½ cups chicken broth
2 tablespoons snipped parsley
1 teaspoon poultry seasoning
12 cups dry bread cubes

In skillet cook bacon till crisp; crumble and set aside. Cook celery and onion in the bacon drippings till tender but not brown. In mixing bowl combine eggs, chicken broth, snipped parsley, poultry seasoning, crumbled bacon, and cooked celery and onion. Add dry bread cubes; toss lightly till well mixed. If desired, add ½ cup additional chicken broth for a moist stuffing. Form mixture into balls, using ½ cup stuffing mixture for each. Bake in greased muffin pans at 325° for 25 to 30 minutes. Makes 12 stuffing balls.

Sauce Veronica

3 tablespoons sugar
1 8-ounce can light seedless
  grapes
¼ cup dry white wine
1 tablespoon cornstarch
¼ teaspoon salt
¼ teaspoon grated orange peel
¼ teaspoon grated lemon peel
2 tablespoons lemon juice

In small heavy saucepan melt sugar over medium heat, stirring constantly, till sugar is deep golden brown. Remove from heat.

Drain grapes, reserving syrup. Heat syrup to boiling; *slowly* stir into caramelized sugar. Cook and stir till dissolved. Combine wine, cornstarch, salt, and grated orange and lemon peels; stir into hot syrup mixture. Cook, stirring constantly, till thickened and bubbly. Add lemon juice and the reserved grapes. Heat just to boiling. Serve with roast chicken or other roast poultry. Makes about 1 cup sauce.

Sweet Cherry and Peach Sauce

1 16-ounce can pitted dark
    sweet cherries
1 8¾-ounce can peaches
2 tablespoons cornstarch
1 tablespoon molasses
2 teaspoons prepared mustard
  Dash salt
¼ cup lemon juice

Drain cherries and peaches; reserve syrups. Halve cherries and chop peaches; set aside. Measure 1½ cups syrup. In saucepan blend syrup and cornstarch. Stir in molasses, mustard, and salt. Cook and stir till thickened and bubbly. Stir in lemon juice and fruits; heat through. Serve with roast poultry. Makes about 3 cups.

Microwave: Prepare fruits as above. Add water to syrup to make 1¾ cups. In a 4-cup glass measure combine cornstarch, molasses, mustard, and salt. Blend in syrup. Cook, uncovered, in countertop microwave oven till heated through, about 2 minutes. Micro-cook for 2 to 3 minutes longer, stirring after each minute. Stir in lemon juice, cherries, and peaches. Micro-cook, uncovered, till sauce is heated through, about 1 minute.

Orange Sauce

1 orange
1 cup water
2 tablespoons red wine vinegar
4 teaspoons sugar
1 cup beef broth
1 tablespoon dry red wine
1 tablespoon cornstarch
2 teaspoons orange liqueur
  Dash bitters

Cut peel from orange. Using sharp knife, remove white membrane and slice peel in julienne strips. Section orange over bowl to catch juice; add orange sections to juice and set aside. In saucepan simmer peel in the water for 15 minutes; drain on paper toweling.

In same saucepan combine vinegar and sugar; cook and stir to a thick syrup. Immediately remove from heat and stir in ¼ *cup* of the beef broth. Simmer for 1 minute, stirring till combined. Add the remaining beef broth. Blend wine into cornstarch; stir into broth mixture. Add orange sections with juice, cooked peel, orange liqueur, and bitters. Heat to boiling. Serve with roast duckling or other roast poultry. Makes about 1½ cups sauce.

Purple Plum Sauce

1 17-ounce can whole unpitted
    purple plums
¼ teaspoon grated orange peel
3 tablespoons orange juice
2 tablespoons sugar
½ teaspoon Worcestershire sauce
¼ teaspoon ground cinnamon

Drain plums, reserving ¼ cup syrup. Sieve plums. In a saucepan combine sieved plums, the reserved plum syrup, grated orange peel, orange juice, sugar, Worcestershire sauce, and ground cinnamon. Heat to boiling; simmer about 10 minutes. Serve with roast duckling or other roast poultry. Makes 1¼ cups sauce.

Prepare a classic French dish, Canard à l'Orange, ▶ with little fuss. Simply stuff a duckling with a quartered unpeeled orange, roast the bird until tender, and serve with *Orange Sauce.*

Curried Apricot Glaze

¼ cup finely chopped dried
    apricots
2 slices bacon, chopped
¼ cup chopped onion
¾ teaspoon curry powder
1 tablespoon brown sugar
1 teaspoon cornstarch
1 teaspoon instant beef bouillon
    granules
⅛ teaspoon salt

In saucepan combine apricots and 1¼ cups water. Simmer, covered, till tender, about 20 minutes. Do not drain. In saucepan cook bacon, onion, and curry powder over low heat till bacon is crisp and onion is tender, stirring occasionally. Stir in brown sugar, cornstarch, bouillon granules, and salt. Add apricots and liquid; cook and stir till thickened and bubbly. Brush over poultry last 10 to 15 minutes of roasting. Pass remainder as sauce. Makes 1 cup.

Pineapple-Orange Glaze

½ of a 6-ounce can frozen
    pineapple juice concentrate
    (⅓ cup)
¼ cup orange marmalade
2 tablespoons bottled steak sauce

In saucepan combine all ingredients. Cook and stir till heated through. Brush over poultry during last 15 minutes of roasting. Makes ⅔ cup.

Soy-Lemon Basting Sauce

1 tablespoon brown sugar
1 teaspoon cornstarch
2 tablespoons lemon juice
2 tablespoons soy sauce
2 tablespoons water
2 tablespoons sliced green onion
    with tops
1 tablespoon butter *or* margarine
1 clove garlic, minced

In saucepan combine brown sugar and cornstarch. Stir in lemon juice, soy sauce, and water. Add onion, butter, and garlic. Cook and stir till thickened and bubbly. Brush over poultry last 15 minutes of roasting. Makes ⅓ cup.

Spiced Raspberry Glaze

¼ cup red raspberry jelly
1 tablespoon lemon juice
1 tablespoon butter *or* margarine
1½ teaspoons cornstarch
¼ teaspoon salt
    Dash ground cinnamon
1 tablespoon vinegar

In saucepan combine jelly, lemon juice, and butter; heat and stir till jelly melts. Combine cornstarch, salt, and cinnamon; blend in vinegar. Stir into jelly mixture; cook and stir till thickened and bubbly. Brush over poultry last 15 minutes of roasting. Makes ⅓ cup.

Cranberry-Wine Sauce

In saucepan combine one 8-ounce can whole **cranberry sauce,** ¼ cup packed **brown sugar,** 2 tablespoons dry **red wine,** 1 tablespoon **cornstarch,** and 1 teaspoon prepared **mustard.** Cook and stir till slightly thickened and bubbly. Serve with roast poultry. Makes 1¼ cups sauce.

Mushroom Gravy for Roast Birds

Remove roast poultry to platter; keep warm. Pour **pan drippings** into large measuring cup. Skim off fat. Add enough **water** to drippings to make 1½ cups liquid; return to roasting pan. In a screw-top jar combine ½ cup cold *water* with ¼ cup all-purpose **flour;** shake well. Stir flour mixture into pan juices. Cook and stir till thickened and bubbly. Add one 6-ounce can sliced **mushrooms.** Season to taste. Simmer 2 to 3 minutes; stir occasionally. Makes 2 cups.

Cream Gravy for Fried Chicken

Remove fried chicken to platter; keep warm. Reserve 3 tablespoons **drippings** in skillet. In screw-top jar combine ¾ cup **milk,** 3 tablespoons all-purpose **flour,** 1 teaspoon **salt,** and dash **pepper;** shake till well blended. Stir into drippings in skillet. Blend in an additional ¾ cup **milk.** Cook, stirring constantly, till thickened and bubbly. Cook 2 to 3 minutes longer. Makes 1½ cups gravy.

Pan Gravy for Roast Poultry

Remove roast poultry to serving platter; cover to keep warm. Leaving crusty bits in roasting pan, pour **pan drippings** into a large measuring cup. Skim off fat, reserving ¼ cup. Return reserved fat to roasting pan; stir in ¼ cup all-purpose **flour.** Cook and stir over low heat till bubbly. Remove pan from heat. Add **liquid** (water, milk, *or* broth) to drippings to make 2 cups. Add to pan all at once. Cook and stir till thickened and bubbly. Season to taste with **salt** and **pepper.** Makes 2 cups gravy.

Sour Cream Gravy

Remove poultry; keep warm. Pour **pan drippings** into measuring cup. Skim off fat; return 2 tablespoons fat to pan. Blend 1 tablespoon all-purpose **flour** into fat in pan. Add **water** to drippings to make 1 cup; stir into fat-flour mixture with ½ teaspoon **salt.** Cook and stir till bubbly. Blend in ½ cup dairy **sour cream.** Heat without boiling over low heat. Makes 1¼ cups.

To Cook Giblets

Place **giblets,** except liver, in saucepan. Add **water** just to cover; **salt** lightly. Add a few **celery** leaves and **onion** slices, if desired. Cover and simmer till tender, 1 to 2 hours. Add turkey liver for last 20 to 30 minutes *or* add chicken liver last 5 to 10 minutes. Cool giblets in broth; remove and chop. Use giblets and broth in gravy, soup, or stuffing.

Southern Giblet Gravy

Cook ½ pound turkey *or* chicken **giblets** including neck; cool and chop. Reserve broth. Add enough reserved broth to **drippings** from roast bird to make 3 cups. (If making gravy without roasting a bird, use only giblet broth.) In screw-top jar combine ½ cup all-purpose **flour,** *1 cup* of the broth mixture, and dash **pepper;** shake well. In saucepan combine flour mixture and remaining broth. Cook and stir till thickened and bubbly. Stir in giblets and 2 hard-cooked **eggs,** chopped. Heat through. Makes 4 cups.

To Make Pan Gravy

Remove bird to platter and keep warm. Leaving crusty bits in roasting pan, pour fat and juices into a large measuring cup. Skim off fat; reserve fat.

Return reserved fat to roasting pan; stir in flour. Cook, stirring constantly, over very low heat until bubbly. Remove pan from the heat.

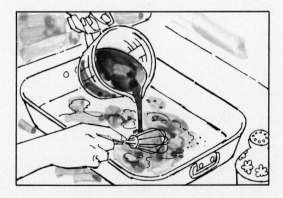

Add liquid to pan juices; stir into fat-flour mixture all at once. Return to heat; cook and stir till thickened and bubbly. Season to taste.

Game Birds

Pheasant with Apples

  ¼ cup all-purpose flour
  1 teaspoon salt
  ¼ teaspoon pepper
  2 2- to 3-pound pheasants, cut up
  6 tablespoons butter *or* margarine
  ¾ cup dry white wine
  ¾ cup light cream
  3 egg yolks
    Sauteed Apples

Combine flour, salt, and pepper in a paper or plastic bag. Add 2 or 3 pheasant pieces at a time; shake to coat. In skillet brown birds lightly in butter. Add wine; simmer, covered, till tender, 45 to 55 minutes. Remove to platter; keep warm. Beat cream with egg yolks. Slowly stir into pan drippings; cook and stir over medium heat just till thickened. (*Do not boil.*) Pour sauce over pheasant. Serve with Sauteed Apples. Makes 4 to 6 servings.

  Sauteed Apples: Add 2 **apples**, cored and cut in wedges, to 3 tablespoons **butter** in medium skillet. Sprinkle with 1 teaspoon **sugar.** Cook, turning often, till lightly browned.

Wild Rice-Stuffed Pheasant

  ½ cup chopped onion
  ¼ cup butter *or* margarine
  ⅔ cup wild rice, rinsed
  1 4½-ounce jar sliced mushrooms, drained
  ½ teaspoon ground sage
  2 2- to 3-pound pheasants
  6 slices bacon

Cook onion in butter. Add rice, 2 cups water, and 1 teaspoon salt. Cover; cook till rice is tender, 35 to 40 minutes. Stir in mushrooms and sage. Rub cavities of birds with salt; stuff lightly with rice. Skewer neck skin to back; tie legs to tail; twist wings under back. Place, breast up, on rack in shallow roasting pan. Lay bacon over birds. Roast in uncovered pan at 350° till tender, 1½ to 2½ hours, depending on size of birds. Makes 4 to 6 servings.

Pheasant in Wine Sauce

  ¼ cup all-purpose flour
  1½ teaspoons paprika
  ½ teaspoon salt
  ⅛ teaspoon pepper
  1 2- to 3-pound pheasant, cut up
  2 tablespoons shortening
  ½ cup dry white wine
  1 3-ounce can sliced mushrooms
  ¼ cup sliced green onion with tops

Combine flour, paprika, salt, and pepper in a paper or plastic bag. Add 2 or 3 pheasant pieces at a time; shake well to coat. In skillet brown pheasant pieces on all sides in hot shortening. Add white wine, undrained mushrooms, and sliced green onion. Cover and simmer till tender, 50 to 60 minutes. Makes 2 or 3 servings.

Roast Stuffed Pheasant

In skillet cook 8 slices **bacon** till crisp. Drain off fat; crumble bacon. In same skillet cook 1 cup chopped **celery** and ¼ cup chopped **onion** in ½ cup **water,** covered, till crisp-tender, 5 to 7 minutes; drain. Combine crumbled bacon, vegetables, 4 cups toasted **bread cubes,** 1 cup **chicken broth,** and ½ teaspoon ground **sage;** toss well. Season cavities of three 2- to 3-pound **pheasants** with **salt;** spoon stuffing lightly into cavities. Skewer neck skin to back. Tie legs to tail. Twist wings under back. Place pheasants, breast up, on rack in shallow roasting pan. Lay 3 uncooked slices **bacon** over *each* bird. Roast in uncovered pan at 350° till tender, 1½ to 2½ hours, depending on size of birds. Serve with **Cranberry-Wine Sauce** (see page 66), if desired. Makes 6 to 8 servings.

Reward the hunter who brings home the pheasants by turning the game into *Pheasant with Apples.* Simmer pheasant pieces in wine, drape them with a creamy sauce, and garnish with *Sauteed Apples.*

Smothered Pheasant

>2 tablespoons all-purpose flour
>½ teaspoon salt
>⅛ teaspoon pepper
>1 2- to 3-pound pheasant, cut up
>2 tablespoons lard *or* shortening
>2 medium onions, sliced
>1 cup water
>¾ cup milk
>2 tablespoons all-purpose flour
>1 teaspoon salt
> Dash pepper
> Paprika

In a paper or plastic bag combine 2 tablespoons flour, ½ teaspoon salt, and ⅛ teaspoon pepper. Add pheasant pieces, a few at a time; shake to coat. In skillet brown pheasant slowly in hot lard. Arrange onions atop pheasant; add 1 cup water. Cover tightly; cook over low heat till tender, 50 to 60 minutes.

Remove pheasant; measure liquid in pan. Add more water, if needed, to make 1 cup liquid; return to pan. In screw-top jar shake milk, 2 tablespoons flour, 1 teaspoon salt, and dash pepper till blended; stir into pan juices. Cook, stirring constantly, till thickened and bubbly. Cook and stir 2 to 3 minutes more. Before serving, sprinkle pheasant with paprika. Pass gravy. Serves 2 or 3.

Partridges in Red Wine

>2 1-pound partridges *or*
> Cornish game hens
>3 tablespoons all-purpose flour
>½ teaspoon salt
>2 tablespoons butter *or* margarine
>1 cup beef broth
>2 tablespoons finely chopped
> onion
>½ cup Burgundy *or* claret

Split birds in half lengthwise. Combine flour and salt; coat birds with mixture. In skillet brown birds slowly in butter. Add broth and onion. Cook, covered, over low heat till tender, 45 to 55 minutes. Remove to serving platter; keep warm. Skim fat from pan drippings. Stir wine into drippings. Over high heat, boil vigorously to reduce liquid to ½ cup, about 10 minutes. Spoon sauce over birds. Makes 2 servings.

Quail with Currant Jelly Sauce

>8 4- to 6-ounce quail
>3 tablespoons butter *or* margarine
>½ cup chicken broth
>½ teaspoon finely shredded
> orange peel
>½ cup orange juice
>⅓ cup currant jelly
>⅛ teaspoon ground ginger
>2 teaspoons lemon juice
>2 teaspoons cornstarch

Tie legs of each quail together; twist wings under back. In skillet brown quail in butter. Season with salt and pepper. Add chicken broth to skillet. Cover and simmer till birds are tender, 25 to 30 minutes. Meanwhile, in small saucepan combine orange peel, orange juice, jelly, and ginger. Heat till jelly melts, stirring occasionally. Blend lemon juice into cornstarch; stir into jelly mixture. Cook and stir till thickened and bubbly; cook 1 to 2 minutes longer. Season to taste. Remove quail to warm platter. Spoon some of the sauce over; pass the remaining sauce. Makes 4 servings.

Savory Quail

>8 4- to 6-ounce quail
>¼ cup all-purpose flour
>1 teaspoon salt
>⅛ teaspoon pepper
>¼ cup butter *or* margarine
>½ cup dry white wine
>2 tablespoons sliced green
> onion with tops
>½ cup light cream
>2 egg yolks
>¼ teaspoon salt

Tie legs of each quail together; twist wings under back. In paper or plastic bag combine flour, 1 teaspoon salt, and pepper. Add quail, 2 or 3 at a time; shake well to coat. In skillet brown quail slowly in butter. Add wine and onion. Cover and simmer till tender, 25 to 30 minutes. Remove quail to platter; keep warm. Reserve ½ cup juices in skillet. Beat cream with egg yolks, ¼ teaspoon salt, and dash pepper; slowly stir into pan juices. Cook and stir till thickened. (*Do not boil.*) Serve sauce over quail. Makes 4 servings.

Broiled Quail

Preheat broiler. Split four 4- to 6-ounce **quail** in half lengthwise. Brush with melted **butter** *or* **margarine**; season with **salt** and **pepper**. Place, skin side up, in broiler pan (no rack). Broil 4 to 5 inches from heat about 5 minutes. Turn; broil 6 to 9 minutes. Brush frequently with melted butter during broiling. Remove to warm serving platter; garnish with **parsley.** Serve with **currant jelly.** Makes 2 servings.

Squab with Apricot Sauce

> 4 12- to 14-ounce squab, halved
>   lengthwise
> ¼ cup butter *or* margarine
> ½ cup chicken broth
> ½ cup apricot nectar
> 2 teaspoons cornstarch

Season squab with salt. In skillet brown squab, skin side down, in butter. Turn; simmer, covered, till tender, about 35 minutes. Remove to platter; keep warm. Combine broth, apricot nectar, and cornstarch. Add to pan drippings. Cook and stir till thickened and bubbly. Pour sauce over birds. Makes 4 servings.

Italian-Style Squab

> 4 12- to 14-ounce squab
> ¼ cup all-purpose flour
> 1½ teaspoons salt
> 2 tablespoons cooking oil
> 1 16-ounce can tomatoes
> 2 medium onions, sliced
> 1 green pepper, sliced
> 1 3-ounce can sliced mushrooms
> 4 sprigs parsley
> 1 clove garlic, minced
> 1 bay leaf

Cut squab in quarters. In plastic bag combine flour and salt. Add 2 or 3 squab pieces at a time; shake to coat. In large skillet brown squab pieces in hot oil. Add undrained tomatoes, onions, green pepper, undrained mushrooms, parsley, garlic, and bay leaf. Cook, covered, over low heat till tender, about 35 minutes. Uncover; cook 10 to 15 minutes more. Remove parsley and bay leaf. Makes 4 servings.

Quail Braised in Tomato Juice

> 4 4- to 6-ounce quail, pigeons,
>   *or* other small game birds
> 1 lemon, halved
>   Parsley
> ¼ cup butter *or* margarine
> 1 cup tomato juice
> 1 cup dry red *or* white wine
> 2 tablespoons butter *or* margarine
> 4 slices buttered toast

Rub birds inside and out with lemon. Season. Place some parsley in each cavity. Tie legs together; twist wings under back. In skillet brown birds well in ¼ cup butter. Add tomato juice; cover and cook slowly till tender, 30 to 45 minutes, basting 2 or 3 times. Remove birds from skillet. Add wine and 2 tablespoons butter to pan drippings; bring to boiling. Place each bird on a slice of toast. Spoon wine sauce over each. Makes 2 servings.

Lemon Squab in a Wok

Dark soy sauce has a more intense flavor than light. You'll find it at an oriental specialty shop—

> 2 12- to 14-ounce squab *or* two
>   1-pound Cornish game hens
> 2 tablespoons dark soy sauce
> ¼ cup peanut *or* cooking oil
> ⅓ cup water
> 2 tablespoons sugar
> 2 tablespoons lemon juice
> 1 teaspoon light soy sauce
> ½ teaspoon cognac *or* brandy
> ¼ teaspoon sesame seed oil
>   (optional)
>   Lemon slices

Rub birds inside and out with dark soy sauce. In wok or skillet brown birds on all sides in hot peanut oil till golden, about 10 minutes. Drain off excess fat. Combine water, sugar, lemon juice, light soy sauce, cognac, and sesame seed oil. Add to wok. Reduce heat; cover and simmer till birds are tender, 45 to 50 minutes. Remove birds; drain on paper toweling. Keep warm. Over high heat, boil pan juices to reduce liquid to ¼ cup, about 5 minutes. Quarter birds or cut in pieces; place on serving platter. Garnish with lemon slices; serve with pan juices. Makes 2 servings.

Cantonese Duck

2 1½- to 2-pound wild ducks
1 orange, cut in wedges
  Celery leaves
½ cup apricot preserves
¼ cup water
1 tablespoon prepared mustard
1 tablespoon soy sauce
1 tablespoon lemon juice
  Hot cooked rice

Rub ducks inside and out with salt. Place orange wedges and a few celery leaves in each cavity. Skewer neck skin to back; tie legs to tail. Twist wings under back. Place, breast up, on rack in shallow roasting pan. Roast in uncovered pan at 400° for 1 to 1½ hours. Cap with foil to prevent excess browning, if needed.

Meanwhile, in saucepan combine apricot preserves, water, mustard, soy, and lemon juice. Heat, stirring constantly. Baste ducks with sauce during last 10 minutes of roasting. Discard stuffing, if desired. Serve ducks on hot rice; pass remaining sauce. Makes 4 servings.

Burgundy-Sauced Wild Ducks

2 1½- to 2-pound wild ducks,
    quartered
2 tablespoons butter *or* margarine
2 tablespoons all-purpose flour
1 cup beef broth
½ cup sliced fresh mushrooms
¼ cup Burgundy
2 tablespoons chopped onion
1 bay leaf
½ teaspoon salt
  Dash pepper
  Snipped parsley

In a large saucepan simmer ducks in small amount of salted water for 20 to 30 minutes; drain. In large skillet brown ducks slowly in butter; transfer to a 12x7½x2-inch baking dish. Blend flour into pan drippings. Stir in broth, mushrooms, Burgundy, onion, bay leaf, salt, and pepper. Cook and stir till thickened and bubbly. Pour sauce over ducks. Cover; bake at 350° till tender, 1¼ to 1½ hours. Remove ducks to platter. Remove bay leaf; skim off fat. Drizzle sauce over ducks; sprinkle with parsley. Makes 4 servings.

Wild Duck à l'Orange

2 1½- to 2-pound wild ducks,
    halved lengthwise
1 medium onion, sliced and
    separated into rings
2 tablespoons butter *or* margarine
2 tablespoons frozen orange juice
    concentrate
2 tablespoons honey
1 tablespoon lemon juice
½ teaspoon ground ginger
¼ teaspoon ground allspice

Place duck halves on a rack in shallow roasting pan. Roast in uncovered pan at 400° till tender, about 1 hour. If necessary, cap with foil to prevent excess browning.

Meanwhile, prepare orange glaze. Cook onion in butter till tender but not brown. Stir in orange juice concentrate, honey, lemon juice, ginger, and allspice. Heat just to boiling. Baste duck with glaze during last 5 to 10 minutes of roasting. Skim fat from pan juices. Serve juices with duck. Makes 4 servings.

Fruit-Stuffed Wild Goose

3½ cups soft bread cubes
1½ cups chopped peeled apple
½ cup chopped onion
½ cup raisins
½ cup butter *or* margarine,
    melted
¾ teaspoon salt
¼ teaspoon ground sage
¼ teaspoon dried rosemary,
    crushed
⅛ teaspoon pepper
1 4- to 6-pound wild goose
3 or 4 slices bacon

Toss together bread cubes, chopped apple, onion, raisins, melted butter or margarine, salt, sage, rosemary, and pepper. Lightly stuff goose with bread mixture; skewer neck skin to back. Tie legs to tail; twist wings under back. Place goose, breast up, on rack in shallow roasting pan. Lay bacon slices over breast. Roast in uncovered pan at 400° till meat thermometer inserted in breast registers 185°, 2 to 3 hours, basting occasionally with drippings. Remove bacon. Makes 4 servings.

Roasting Chart for Game Birds

Take care of your game bird in the field, and you'll maintain the high quality of the meat. As soon as possible, pluck, draw, clean, and cool the bird. And, remove the oil sac at the base of the tail.

Now you're ready to cook. Rinse the bird and pat dry with paper toweling.

Rub inside of cavities with salt. Spoon stuffing loosely into bird, if desired. Pull the neck skin to the back of bird and fasten securely with a small skewer. Tie legs securely to tail. Twist wing tips under back.

Place bird, breast side up, on a rack in shallow roasting pan. *Except* for wild duck, brush bird with melted butter or cooking oil, or lay uncooked bacon slices over the breast. Roast in uncovered pan until bird is tender, according to the chart below. Baste bird occasionally with pan drippings. Place foil loosely over top of bird to prevent excess browning, if necessary.

Cooking time may vary with the size and age of the bird. Young, tender birds are more suitable for roasting.

Game Birds	Ready-to-Cook Weight	Oven Temp.	Roasting Time	Number of Servings	Special Instructions
Wild Duck	1½-2 lbs.	400°	1-1½ hrs.	Two	Stuff loosely with quartered onions and apples; discard after roasting, if desired. Do not brush with oil.
Wild Goose	2-4 lbs. 4-6 lbs.	400°	1½-2 hrs. 2-3 hrs.	Two Four	Stuff loosely with quartered onions and apples; discard after roasting, if desired. Baste often.
Pheasant	2-3 lbs.	350°	1½-2½ hrs.	Two or Three	Place bacon slices over breast.
Quail	4-6 oz.	400°	30-45 min.	One-Half	Place bacon slices over breast.
Squab	12-14 oz.	400°	40-50 min.	One	Place bacon slices over breast.
Partridge	½-1 lb.	450°	30-45 min.	One	Place bacon slices over breast.

Entertaining Specialties

Giving a party is a great way to
celebrate friendship, and
every party-goer enjoys an enticing
appetizer or a distinctive
dinner entrée. Since party groups
come in all sizes, this
selection of recipes accommodates
intimate twosomes as well
as crowd-size get-togethers or
neighborhood potluck suppers.
   The recipes in this chapter were
chosen to help you prepare
a memorable specialty, no matter
what the circumstance. And,
the circumstances certainly are
varied, from casual meals—
perhaps planned on an impulse—
to formal, elegant dinners
or special luncheons. Outstanding
appetizers, main-course
dishes, and buffet dishes will help
you meet these occasions.

Excellent selections for entertaining,
Chicken Veronique and *Chicken
and Broccoli Crepes* can't help but please
luncheon or dinner guests (see
recipes, page 82). Whether you prefer to
entertain simply or formally,
these entrées harmonize with your style.

Appealing Appetizers

Rumaki

9 slices bacon, halved
9 chicken livers, halved
   (about 9 ounces)
9 water chestnuts, halved
¼ cup soy sauce
1 tablespoon sugar
⅛ teaspoon ground ginger

Partially cook bacon; drain on paper toweling. Combine remaining ingredients. Cover and marinate about 20 minutes; drain. Wrap 1 chicken liver piece and 1 water chestnut piece in a half-slice of bacon. Secure with a wooden pick. Place appetizers in 8x8x2-inch baking pan. Bake at 450° till bacon is crisp, 10 to 12 minutes. Drain appetizers on paper toweling. Serve hot. Makes 18 appetizers.

Chicken Liver Paté

1 pound chicken livers
2 tablespoons butter or margarine
3 tablespoons mayonnaise or salad
   dressing
2 tablespoons lemon juice
2 tablespoons butter or
   margarine, softened
1 tablespoon finely chopped onion
8 to 10 drops bottled hot pepper
   sauce
½ teaspoon dry mustard
½ teaspoon salt
   Dash pepper
   Assorted crackers

In heavy saucepan cook livers, covered, in 2 tablespoons butter, stirring occasionally, till no longer pink. Put livers through a meat grinder; blend with mayonnaise or salad dressing, lemon juice, 2 tablespoons softened butter, onion, hot pepper sauce, dry mustard, salt, and pepper. Place mixture in 2-cup mold. Cover; chill several hours. Carefully unmold. If desired, garnish with chopped hard-cooked egg, snipped chives, or snipped parsley. Serve with assorted crackers. Makes about 2 cups spread.

Taco Chicken Wings

½ cup all-purpose flour
1 envelope taco seasoning mix
3 pounds chicken wings, tips
   removed and cut at joints
   (about 32 chicken pieces)
6 tablespoons butter or margarine
1 cup crushed corn chips

In paper or plastic bag combine flour and taco seasoning mix. Add 2 or 3 chicken pieces at a time; shake to coat. Melt butter in 15½x10½x1-inch baking pan. Place chicken in pan, turning once to butter surfaces, then roll in corn chips and return to pan. Bake at 350° for 40 to 45 minutes. Makes about 32 appetizers.

Appetizer Chicken Fondue

3 whole large chicken breasts
¼ cup soy sauce
2 tablespoons dry sherry
1 tablespoon sugar
1 tablespoon vinegar
¼ teaspoon ground ginger
6 slices bacon
   Cooking oil

In skillet bring chicken breasts and 2 cups salted water to boiling. Reduce heat; cover and simmer till tender, about 20 minutes. Remove chicken; cool slightly. Discard skin and bones; cut meat in ¾-inch cubes. Combine soy, sherry, sugar, vinegar, and ginger. Add chicken. Cover and let stand 30 minutes at room temperature; turn occasionally. Drain well.

Cut each bacon slice in thirds crosswise, then in half lengthwise, making 36 pieces. Wrap one piece around each chicken cube, securing with end of bamboo skewer. Chill thoroughly, at least 1 hour, before cooking.

Pour cooking oil into metal fondue cooker to no more than ½ capacity or to depth of 2 inches. Heat over range to 375°. Add 1 teaspoon salt. Transfer cooker to fondue burner. Fry chicken cubes in hot oil till the bacon is cooked, about 1 minute. Makes 36 appetizers.

Arrange your next appetizer buffet around *Taco Chicken Wings.* Coated with Mexican-style seasonings and crunchy corn chips, these peppy finger foods make a tasty and unique focal point.

Chicken Chinese Egg Rolls

Purchase egg roll skins at an oriental food shop or a large supermarket—

> 2 5-ounce cans boned chicken, drained and chopped, *or* 1 cup chopped cooked chicken
> 1 4-ounce can chopped mushrooms, drained and finely chopped
> ½ cup chopped celery
> 2 teaspoons soy sauce
> 1 teaspoon curry powder
> 8 egg roll skins
> Fat for frying

Combine first 5 ingredients. Lay one skin diagonally in front of you; spread small amount of filling in strip across center to within ½ inch of points. Fold skin into an envelope by bringing up bottom point, then folding in points from each side. Roll up, moistening underside of last point. Repeat with remaining skins. Fry in deep hot fat (375°) for 2 to 3 minutes. Cut in thirds. Makes 24 appetizers.

Deviled Chicken Livers

> 1 pound chicken livers (about 16)
> 3 tablespoons butter *or* margarine, melted
> ⅔ cup fine dry bread crumbs
> 2 teaspoons butter *or* margarine
> 2 tablespoons Dijon-style mustard
> 1 tablespoon catsup
> 2 teaspoons Worcestershire sauce
> ½ teaspoon onion powder
> Dash cayenne

Dip chicken livers in the 3 tablespoons melted butter; coat with the bread crumbs. Place in greased shallow pan. Broil 6 inches from heat till chicken livers are tender, about 3 minutes on each side. Be careful not to overcook.

Melt the 2 teaspoons butter or margarine; stir in Dijon-style mustard, catsup, Worcestershire sauce, onion powder, and cayenne. Heat sauce mixture just to boiling. Serve chicken livers on wooden picks with sauce for dipping. Makes about 16 appetizers.

Party Chicken-Hamwiches

12 slices firm-textured whole
    wheat bread
  Butter *or* margarine, softened
6 slices firm-textured white
    bread
  Dijon-style mustard
1 4-ounce package thinly sliced
    ham
1 cup chopped cooked chicken *or*
    turkey
2 hard-cooked eggs, chopped
¼ cup mayonnaise
2 tablespoons finely chopped
    celery
2 tablespoons sweet pickle relish
1 tablespoon sliced green onion
    with tops
1 teaspoon lemon juice
¼ teaspoon salt

Spread one side of whole wheat bread slices with butter; spread one side of white bread slices with mustard. Trim crusts. Divide ham among six slices wheat bread. Top with white bread, mustard side down. Combine remaining ingredients. Spread about ¼ cup chicken mixture over each slice white bread. Cover each with slice of wheat bread, buttered side down, making 6 sandwiches. Quarter sandwiches diagonally. Makes 24 party sandwiches.

Chicken Pinwheels

2 5-ounce cans chicken spread
¼ cup finely chopped pimiento
½ teaspoon prepared mustard
¼ teaspoon curry powder
1 unsliced loaf white sandwich
    bread
  Butter *or* margarine, softened

Combine chicken spread, pimiento, mustard, and curry. Trim crusts from bread. Cut bread in nine *lengthwise* slices about ¼ inch thick. Spread each long slice with butter and 2 tablespoons chicken mixture. Roll up jelly-roll fashion, starting at short side. Seal with softened butter. Wrap in foil and chill.

To serve, cut in ⅜-inch slices. (Or, make sandwiches ahead; freeze. Cut while frozen; cover and thaw before serving.) Makes 78.

Sesame-Chicken Balls

2 5-ounce cans boned chicken,
    drained and finely chopped
¼ cup mayonnaise *or* salad
    dressing
2 tablespoons finely chopped
    pimiento
1 tablespoon finely chopped onion
1 tablespoon prepared mustard
4 drops bottled hot pepper sauce
¼ cup toasted sesame seed

Combine chicken, salad dressing, pimiento, onion, mustard, and hot pepper sauce. Mix until thoroughly blended. Form into balls, using about 1 teaspoon mixture for each. Chill thoroughly, about 1 hour. Roll chilled balls in sesame seed. Makes 36 balls.

Miniature Chicken Puffs

2 tablespoons butter *or* margarine
¼ cup boiling water
¼ cup all-purpose flour
1 egg
¼ cup shredded Swiss cheese
2 cups finely chopped cooked
    chicken *or* turkey
¼ cup finely chopped celery
¼ cup mayonnaise *or* salad
    dressing
2 tablespoons finely chopped
    pimiento
2 tablespoons dry white wine
½ teaspoon salt
  Dash pepper

In saucepan melt butter or margarine in the boiling water. Add flour and dash salt; stir vigorously. Cook over medium-low heat, stirring constantly and vigorously, till mixture forms a ball that does not separate. Remove from heat and cool for 2 to 3 minutes.

Add egg and beat vigorously till smooth; stir in Swiss cheese. Drop level teaspoonfuls of dough onto greased baking sheet. Bake at 400° about 20 minutes. Remove puffs from oven; cool and split. Combine remaining ingredients. Fill each puff with about 2 teaspoons chicken mixture. (Unfilled puffs may be kept in the freezer. Fill frozen baked puffs without thawing.) Makes about 30 appetizers.

Turkey Spread

2 cups ground cooked turkey
¼ cup chopped walnuts
¼ cup snipped parsley
2 tablespoons finely chopped
    green onion with tops
2 teaspoons lemon juice
1 teaspoon Worcestershire sauce
¾ to 1 cup mayonnaise
    Assorted crackers

In mixing bowl combine turkey, nuts, parsley, onion, lemon juice, and Worcestershire. Blend in mayonnaise till desired consistency. Cover; chill. Serve with crackers. Makes 2 cups.

Turkey in Sour Cream

2 cups cooked turkey *or* chicken
    cut in thin strips
¼ cup thinly sliced green onion
    with tops
¾ cup dairy sour cream
2 tablespoons dry sherry
1 tablespoon sugar
¾ teaspoon salt
½ teaspoon celery seed
¼ teaspoon dillseed
    Dash pepper
    Paprika
    Assorted crackers

Combine turkey and onion. Blend together sour cream, sherry, sugar, salt, celery seed, dillseed, pepper, and ¼ cup water. Toss with turkey mixture. Cover and chill. Sprinkle with paprika. Serve with crackers. Makes 2 cups.

Cashew-Chicken Appetizers

Remove skin and bones from 2 whole **chicken breasts.** Split in half lengthwise; cut meat in 1½-inch strips. Finely chop 7½ ounces **cashew nuts** (1½ cups). Set aside. In small bowl combine ¼ cup **cornstarch** and ½ teaspoon **sugar.** Stir in 2 slightly beaten **egg whites** and 1 teaspoon **cognac** *or* **brandy.** Dip chicken pieces in egg white mixture, then in cashew nuts. Fry chicken in deep hot fat (375°) till golden, about 45 seconds. Drain pieces thoroughly on paper toweling. Makes about 30 appetizers.

Sour Cream-Chicken Dip

1 cup dairy sour cream
1 5-ounce can boned chicken,
    drained
1 2-ounce can chopped mushrooms,
    drained
1 to 2 teaspoons curry powder
½ cup finely chopped peanuts
    Vegetable dippers, crackers, *or*
    potato chips

In blender container combine sour cream, chicken, mushrooms, and curry. Cover; blend till smooth; chill. At serving time, stir in peanuts. Serve with dippers. Makes 1½ cups.

Chicken Madrilene

1 envelope unflavored gelatin
1 cup chilled tomato juice
1½ cups water
2 chicken bouillon cubes
2 tablespoons dry sherry
    Dash pepper
    Snipped chives
    Lemon wedges

Soften gelatin in *half* of the tomato juice. Bring water and bouillon cubes to boiling, stirring till dissolved. Add gelatin mixture; stir till gelatin is dissolved. Add remaining juice, sherry, and pepper. Chill, stirring 2 or 3 times, till partially set. Chill till firm. Spoon into serving dishes. Trim with chives; serve with lemon wedges. Makes 4 to 6 servings.

Chicken-Cucumber Soup

1 10¾-ounce can condensed cream
    of chicken soup
⅓ cup dairy sour cream
1 6-ounce can vegetable juice
    cocktail (¾ cup)
¾ cup cold water
⅓ cup finely chopped, seeded
    cucumber
¼ teaspoon dried rosemary,
    crushed

In bowl blend soup and sour cream until smooth; stir in remaining ingredients. Chill 3 hours. Serve in chilled bowls. Serves 3 or 4.

Guest-Pleasing Entrées

Chicken Saltimbocca

3 whole large chicken breasts,
   skinned, boned, and halved
   lengthwise
6 thin slices boiled ham
6 slices process Swiss cheese
1 medium tomato, peeled, seeded,
   and chopped
   Dried sage, crushed
⅓ cup fine dry bread crumbs
2 tablespoons grated Parmesan
   cheese
2 tablespoons snipped parsley
¼ cup butter or margarine, melted

Place chicken, boned side up, between two pieces clear plastic wrap. Working out from the center, pound each lightly with meat mallet to 5½x5½ inches. Remove wrap. Place a ham slice and a cheese slice on each cutlet, cutting to fit within ¼ inch of edges. Top with some tomato; sprinkle lightly with sage. Fold in sides; roll up jelly-roll fashion, pressing to seal well. Combine crumbs, Parmesan, and parsley. Dip chicken in butter, then roll in crumbs. Bake in shallow baking pan at 350° for 40 to 45 minutes. Remove to platter. Blend mixture remaining in pan till smooth; serve over chicken. Serves 6.

Microwave: Prepare chicken rolls as above, except place in 12x7½x2-inch glass baking dish. Cook, covered, in a countertop microwave oven till chicken is tender, about 10 minutes, turning dish once. Serve chicken as above.

Layered Beef and Chicken Bake

Run cold water over beef from one 3-ounce package sliced **dried beef;** drain. Arrange in 12x7½x2-inch baking dish. Remove skin and bones from 3 whole large **chicken breasts;** halve lengthwise. Place atop beef. Place 6 slices **bacon** atop chicken. Bake at 350° for 30 minutes. Combine one 10¾-ounce can condensed **cream of mushroom soup** and 1 cup dairy **sour cream;** pour over chicken. Bake 25 minutes more. Makes 6 servings.

Chicken Jubilee

6 whole small chicken breasts,
   skinned and boned
1 20-ounce can pineapple slices
1 cup diced fully cooked ham
2 tablespoons chopped onion
2 tablespoons butter or margarine
¼ cup crushed crackers
¼ teaspoon ground ginger
¼ cup butter or margarine
¼ cup chicken broth
2 tablespoons vinegar
½ teaspoon salt
1 tablespoon cornstarch
1 8¾-ounce can pitted dark sweet
   cherries, drained
¼ cup brandy

Place chicken, boned side up, between two pieces clear plastic wrap. Pound out from the center with meat mallet to ¼ inch thickness. Remove wrap. Drain pineapple, reserving ½ cup syrup. Chop 4 of the slices; cook with ham and onion in 2 tablespoons butter. Add cracker crumbs and ginger; mix well. Divide ham mixture evenly among chicken pieces. Fold in sides and roll up jelly-roll fashion. Skewer shut.

In a skillet brown chicken rolls slowly on all sides in ¼ cup butter. And chicken broth, vinegar, and salt. Cover; cook till chicken is tender, about 30 minutes. Remove chicken to serving plate; keep warm. Blend reserved pineapple syrup into cornstarch; stir into broth mixture. Cook and stir till thickened and bubbly. Stir in remaining pineapple slices and cherries; heat through. Pour fruit sauce into a heat-proof dish. Heat brandy in ladle or small pan; flame at the table and pour over sauce. Stir brandy into sauce when flame dies down. Serve sauce with chicken. Makes 6 servings.

Splurge on glamour and flavor with our adaptation ▶ of a classic Italian recipe, *Chicken Saltimbocca.* Ham, Swiss cheese, and fresh tomato are rolled up inside chicken breasts for a high-style entrée.

Saucy Chicken Livers

½ cup chopped onion
2 tablespoons butter *or* margarine
1 pound chicken livers, halved
½ teaspoon salt
    Dash pepper
1 cup dairy sour cream
1 tablespoon all-purpose flour
    Toast points
2 tablespoons snipped parsley

In skillet cook onion in butter till tender. Add chicken livers, salt, and pepper; mix well. Cook till livers are just barely pink. Blend together sour cream and flour; add to livers. Heat through but do not boil. Serve over toast; sprinkle with parsley. Makes 4 servings.

Microwave: In 1-quart glass casserole cook onion in butter in countertop microwave oven till tender, about 2 minutes. Add livers, salt, and pepper; mix well. Micro-cook, covered, till just barely pink, about 6 minutes, stirring after 3 minutes. Combine sour cream and flour; add to livers. Micro-cook, uncovered, till heated through but not boiling, about 2 minutes; stir after 1 minute. Serve as above.

Chicken Veronique

Classic chicken dish pictured on page 74—

1 2½- to 3-pound broiler-fryer
    chicken, cut up
1 lemon, halved
¼ cup butter *or* margarine
⅓ cup dry white wine
    Paprika
1 teaspoon cornstarch
1 cup seedless green grapes

Rub chicken well with the lemon; sprinkle with salt. In skillet brown chicken slowly in hot butter about 10 minutes, turning frequently. Add wine; spoon wine-butter mixture over chicken. Cover; simmer till tender, 30 to 40 minutes. Remove chicken to platter. Sprinkle generously with paprika; keep warm. Skim off fat from pan juices. Measure juices; add water, if needed, to make ¾ cup. Return to pan. Blend 1 tablespoon cold water into cornstarch; stir into juices. Cook and stir till bubbly. Add grapes and heat through. Spoon over chicken. Garnish with lemon slices, if desired. Makes 4 servings.

Chicken-Apricot Fondue

½ cup dairy sour cream
⅓ cup apricot jam
4 teaspoons Dijon-style mustard
1 cup pancake mix
1 tablespoon sugar
¼ teaspoon ground ginger
¾ cup milk
    Cooking oil
3 whole large chicken breasts,
    skinned, boned, and cut in
    ¾-inch cubes

Combine sour cream, jam, and mustard. Combine pancake mix, sugar, and ginger. Add milk; beat smooth. Pour oil into metal fondue cooker to no more than ½ capacity or to depth of 2 inches. Heat over range to 375°. Add 1 teaspoon salt. Transfer cooker to fondue burner. Spear chicken cube with fondue fork. Dip in batter; let excess drip off. Fry in hot oil till golden, 1½ to 2 minutes. Transfer to dinner fork; dip in jam mixture. Makes 4 or 5 servings.

Chicken and Broccoli Crepes

Special-occasion crepes shown on page 74—

For crepes, combine 1 beaten **egg,** 1 cup **milk,** and 1 tablespoon melted **butter.** Add 1 cup all-purpose **flour;** beat smooth. Lightly grease a 6-inch skillet; heat. Pour 2 tablespoons batter into skillet; lift pan and tilt till batter covers bottom. Return to heat. Brown crepe on *1 side only.* To remove, invert pan over paper toweling. Repeat, making 12 crepes. Set aside.

For sauce, melt 6 tablespoons **butter.** Blend in 6 tablespoons all-purpose **flour** and dash **salt.** Add 3 cups **milk** all at once. Cook and stir till thick and bubbly. Blend in ½ cup shredded sharp **American cheese** (2 ounces) and ¼ cup dry **white wine.** Remove ½ cup of the sauce; set aside. Stir one 2½-ounce jar sliced **mushrooms,** drained, into remaining sauce.

For filling, combine 2 cups finely chopped cooked **chicken** *or* **turkey;** one 10-ounce package frozen chopped **broccoli,** cooked and drained; and reserved sauce. Spoon about ¼ cup filling on unbrowned side of each crepe. Roll up jelly-roll fashion. Arrange, seam down, in chafing dish. Pour sauce over. Cover; cook over low heat till bubbly. Makes 6 servings.

Chicken Breasts Amandine

¼ cup all-purpose flour
1½ teaspoons salt
½ teaspoon paprika
⅛ teaspoon pepper
2 tablespoons butter *or* margarine
3 tablespoons dry sherry
2 whole large chicken breasts,
    halved lengthwise (2½ pounds)
⅓ to ½ cup sliced almonds

Combine flour, salt, paprika, and pepper. Melt butter; remove from heat. Stir in sherry. Coat chicken with flour mixture, then dip both sides in butter mixture. Sprinkle both sides of chicken with almonds; pat to stick. Place chicken, skin side up, in greased shallow baking pan. Bake, covered, at 375° for 20 minutes. Uncover; bake till chicken is golden, 20 to 25 minutes longer. Do not turn. Makes 4 servings.

Chicken Kiev

4 whole large chicken breasts,
    skinned, boned, and halved
    lengthwise (3 pounds)
2 tablespoons snipped parsley
1 tablespoon chopped green onion
    with tops
1 ¼-pound stick butter, well
    chilled
2 beaten eggs
½ cup all-purpose flour
½ cup fine dry bread crumbs
    Fat for frying

Place chicken, boned side up, between two pieces clear plastic wrap. Pound out from center with meat mallet to ⅛-inch thickness. Remove wrap. Sprinkle chicken with parsley and onion; season with salt. Cut butter into 8 sticks, each about 2½ inches long. Place 1 stick on each piece of chicken. Fold in sides; roll up jelly-roll fashion, pressing ends to seal. Combine eggs and 2 tablespoons water. Coat chicken with flour, then dip in egg mixture. Roll in crumbs. Cover; chill at least 1 hour. Fry in deep hot fat (375°) till golden, about 5 minutes. (Or, brown cold chicken rolls in skillet on all sides in ¼ cup hot butter about 5 minutes. Transfer to 12x7½x 2-inch baking dish. Bake at 400° for 15 to 18 minutes.) Makes 8 servings.

Party Chicken and Vegetables

6 whole small chicken breasts
1 16-ounce can whole small
    carrots, drained
1 9-ounce package frozen
    artichoke hearts, cooked,
    drained, and halved
1 8-ounce can boiled onions,
    drained
¼ cup butter *or* margarine
⅓ cup all-purpose flour
¾ teaspoon salt
2½ cups milk
1 cup shredded sharp American
    cheese (4 ounces)
½ cup mayonnaise
¼ cup dry sherry
¾ cup soft bread crumbs (1 slice)
1 tablespoon butter, melted
½ teaspoon paprika

In large skillet bring chicken and 2 cups salted water to boiling. Cover; simmer till tender, about 20 minutes. Remove chicken; cool slightly. Discard skin and bones; cube meat. Arrange chicken and vegetables in a 12x7½x2-inch baking dish; set aside. In saucepan melt ¼ cup butter; blend in flour and salt. Add milk all at once. Cook and stir till thickened and bubbly. Cook 2 minutes more; remove from heat. Stir in cheese, mayonnaise, and sherry. Pour over chicken and vegetables. Sprinkle with mixture of bread crumbs, melted butter, and paprika. Bake at 350° till heated through, about 25 minutes. Makes 8 servings.

Microwave: Place chicken in 12x7½x2-inch glass baking dish. Cook, covered, in countertop microwave oven till tender, about 14 minutes; turn chicken over and rearrange twice. Remove chicken; cool slightly. Drain off juices. Discard skin and bones; cube meat. Arrange chicken and vegetables in same baking dish. In 1½-quart glass bowl micro-melt ¼ cup butter 30 to 40 seconds. Blend in flour and salt; add milk. Micro-cook, uncovered, for 1 minute; stir. Micro-cook till thick and bubbly, 4 to 5 minutes; stir every 30 seconds. Stir in cheese, mayonnaise, and sherry; pour over chicken. Micro-cook, covered, till hot, 12 to 15 minutes; give dish a half turn during cooking. Sprinkle with mixture of crumbs, melted butter, and paprika. Micro-cook, uncovered, for 30 seconds.

Paella

¼ cup all-purpose flour
1 2½- to 3-pound broiler-fryer
    chicken, cut up
2 tablespoons olive oil *or*
    cooking oil
2½ cups chicken broth
2 medium onions, quartered
2 carrots, sliced (¾ cup)
⅔ cup regular rice
½ cup chopped celery with leaves
¼ cup chopped pimiento
1 clove garlic, minced
½ teaspoon salt
½ teaspoon dried oregano, crushed
¼ teaspoon ground saffron
12 ounces fresh *or* frozen shelled
    shrimp
12 small fresh clams in shells,
    washed
1 9-ounce package frozen
    artichoke hearts

Combine flour, 1 teaspoon salt, and dash pepper; coat chicken. In 4-quart Dutch oven brown chicken in hot oil about 15 minutes. Drain off fat. Add broth, onions, carrots, rice, celery, pimiento, garlic, salt, oregano, and saffron. Cover; simmer for 30 minutes. Add shrimp, clams, and artichokes. Simmer, covered, 15 to 20 minutes longer. Makes 6 to 8 servings.

Coq au Vin

Cook 2 cups fresh **mushrooms,** sliced, in 2 tablespoons **butter;** set aside. In skillet cook 4 slices **bacon,** cut up, and 2 tablespoons chopped **onion;** remove. Add one cut-up 2½-to 3-pound broiler-fryer **chicken.** Brown slowly in drippings; remove. Add 8 **shallots** *or* small whole **onions;** ½ cup chopped **carrots;** 1 clove **garlic,** minced; and 2 tablespoons **cognac** *or* **brandy.** Cook 3 minutes. Wrap 3 or 4 sprigs **parsley,** 2 or 3 sprigs **celery leaves,** 1 **bay leaf,** and ¼ teaspoon dried **thyme,** crushed, in cheesecloth. Set in 2-quart casserole. Layer chicken, vegetables, and mushrooms in casserole. In same skillet bring 2 cups red **Burgundy** to boiling, stirring to loosen crusty bits. Pour into casserole. Cover; bake at 350° about 2 hours. Remove cheesecloth bag. Makes 4 servings.

Chicken Country Captain

½ cup chopped onion
½ cup chopped green pepper
1 clove garlic, minced
2 tablespoons butter *or* margarine
1 28-ounce can tomatoes, cut up
¼ cup dried currants
¼ cup snipped parsley
2 to 3 teaspoons curry powder
1 teaspoon ground mace
1 teaspoon salt
⅛ teaspoon pepper
• • •
⅓ cup all-purpose flour
1 teaspoon salt
¼ teaspoon pepper
¼ teaspoon paprika
2 2½- to 3-pound broiler-fryer
    chickens, cut up
2 tablespoons cooking oil
2 tablespoons cold water
1 tablespoon cornstarch
    Hot cooked rice
¼ cup sliced almonds (optional)

In large saucepan cook onion, green pepper, and garlic in butter till tender but not brown. Stir in undrained tomatoes, currants, parsley, curry, mace, 1 teaspoon salt, and ⅛ teaspoon pepper. Cook, uncovered, for 15 minutes.

In paper or plastic bag combine flour, 1 teaspoon salt, ¼ teaspoon pepper, and paprika. Add chicken pieces, 2 or 3 at a time; shake to coat. Lightly brown chicken pieces on all sides in hot oil about 15 minutes. Arrange chicken in 13x9x2-inch baking dish; top with tomato mixture. Cover and bake at 325° till chicken is tender, about 1 hour.

Remove chicken from baking dish; keep warm. Skim excess fat from sauce; transfer sauce to a medium saucepan. Blend cold water into cornstarch; stir into sauce. Cook and stir till thickened and bubbly. Serve chicken and sauce over rice. Garnish with almonds, if desired. Makes 8 to 10 servings.

A colonial Southern favorite, *Chicken Country* ▶
Captain has been passed down through generations of good cooks. The recipe is popular along the coast of the Carolinas, especially in Charleston.

Orange-Tarragon Chicken

1 2½- to 3-pound broiler-fryer
    chicken, cut up
1 teaspoon salt
1 teaspoon paprika
2 tablespoons cooking oil
1 teaspoon grated orange peel
1 cup orange juice
1 teaspoon sugar
½ teaspoon dried tarragon,
    crushed
1 tablespoon cold water
2 teaspoons cornstarch

Sprinkle chicken with salt and paprika. In 12-inch skillet brown chicken slowly in hot oil about 15 minutes, turning to brown evenly. Combine orange peel, juice, sugar, and tarragon; pour over chicken. Cover; cook over low heat till tender, 25 to 35 minutes. Remove to platter; keep warm. Skim excess fat from pan drippings. Blend cold water into cornstarch; stir into pan drippings. Cook and stir till bubbly. Pour over chicken. Makes 4 servings.

Patty shells make an attractive base for *Mushroom Creamed Chicken.* Buy the frozen patty shells, then simply pop them into a hot oven and bake.

Classic Chicken à la King

3 egg yolks
¼ cup butter, softened
½ teaspoon paprika
1 cup fresh mushrooms, thinly
    sliced
¼ cup chopped green pepper
2 tablespoons butter *or* margarine
2 tablespoons all-purpose flour
2 cups light cream
3 cups cooked chicken *or* turkey
    cut in pieces
2 tablespoons dry sherry
1 tablespoon lemon juice
1 teaspoon onion juice
2 tablespoons chopped pimiento
  Toast points *or* baked patty
  shells

In bowl blend egg yolks, softened butter, and paprika; set aside. Cook mushrooms and green pepper in 2 tablespoons butter till tender; push vegetables to one side. Blend flour and ¾ teaspoon salt into butter. Stir in cream; cook and stir till thick and bubbly. Add chicken and heat through; stir occasionally. Add sherry, lemon juice, and onion juice. Add yolk mixture all at once; blend well. Immediately remove from heat. Stir in pimiento. Serve at once over toast or in shells. Makes 6 to 8 servings.

Mushroom Creamed Chicken

In large saucepan place one 2½- to 3-pound whole broiler-fryer **chicken,** 3 sprigs **celery leaves,** and 2 teaspoons **salt;** cover with 4 cups **water.** Simmer, covered, about 30 minutes. Drain, straining stock. Reserve 1½ cups; chill remainder for another use. Cool chicken slightly. Discard skin and bones; cut meat in strips.

Cook ½ cup chopped **celery** and ½ cup chopped **onion** in ½ cup **butter.** Add ½ cup sliced fresh **mushrooms;** cook 1 to 2 minutes. Blend in ⅓ cup all-purpose **flour.** Add reserved stock and 1 cup light **cream;** cook and stir till bubbly. Add chicken; one 8-ounce can **water chestnuts,** drained and sliced; ¼ cup dry **sherry;** 2 tablespoons snipped **parsley;** ¼ teaspoon **salt;** and dash **white pepper.** Cook 2 minutes. Serve in 6 baked **patty shells;** top with 2 tablespoons sliced **almonds,** toasted. Serves 6.

Turkey-Cranberry Aspic

Soften 1 envelope **unflavored gelatin** in ⅓ cup **cranberry juice cocktail;** stir over low heat till gelatin is dissolved. With a fork, break up sauce in one 16-ounce can whole **cranberry sauce.** Stir in dissolved gelatin mixture; blend in ½ cup **mayonnaise** *or* **salad dressing.** Whip ½ cup **whipping cream** just to soft peaks. Fold into gelatin mixture with ½ cup chopped **celery.** Pour into a 9x9x2-inch pan. Chill till almost

firm. Carefully place 6 slices cooked **turkey** cut ¼ inch thick atop almost-firm gelatin; trim to fit, if needed.

Meanwhile, soften 1½ teaspoons **unflavored gelatin** in 1½ cups **chicken broth;** stir over low heat till gelatin is dissolved. Add 1 drop **yellow food coloring.** Cool. Carefully pour gelatin-broth mixture over and around turkey slices. Chill till gelatin mixture is firm. To serve, cut in 6 portions. Serve portions on **lettuce leaves,** if desired. Makes 6 servings.

Wine Selection Guide

Serving Wine: Choosing the right wine to serve with poultry needn't be confusing. There are no hard and fast rules—your own preference is the most important consideration. Here are some guidelines to help you enjoy wine to the fullest.

In general, light, delicate dishes call for light-flavored wines that do not overwhelm the food. These subtle white and red dinner wines can be dry, tart, or sweet. Hearty, zesty dishes seem to demand rich, full-flavored wines. Predominately dry and robust, these vibrant wines include most of the red dinner wines. They awaken the palate and enhance the flavor of rich or highly seasoned foods. Rosé wines, ranging in flavor from sweet to slightly

tart, can be delightful companions to delicate or spicy poultry entrées.

Choose wine to fit the circumstance. Many inexpensive wines are suitable for everyday or company meals. But, you may want to reserve more expensive wines to complement a special meal or elegant occasion.

Cooking with Wine: Wine enhances the natural flavors of poultry and game birds. The alcohol evaporates, leaving just the subtle flavor of wine. Use dry wines in main dishes, or use the same type of wine you ordinarily would serve with the food at the table. But gourmet-wise or not, feel free to experiment in a recipe by interchanging wines with similar characteristics.

Wines	Serving Temperature	Best With
Light-Flavored Wines White Burgundy/Chablis White Bordeaux Dry Sauterne Rhine Beaujolais Light Red Bordeaux	Chilled (45° to 50°)	Simply prepared fried, broiled, and roast poultry; light stews and casseroles; mild game birds (pheasant, quail); cold salads and sandwiches; creamed dishes and poultry in delicate sauces (use white wines in light-colored creamed mixtures)
Full-Flavored Wines Red Burgundy Red Bordeaux or Claret Chianti Red Rhône	Cool room temperature (60° to 70°)	Hearty, flavorful casseroles, stews, and baked dishes; poultry in zesty sauces or with rich gravies; barbecued poultry; goose; strong-flavored game birds (wild duck)
Rosé Wine		Most poultry dishes

Chicken Dijon

>   4 whole medium chicken breasts,
>   skinned, boned, and halved
>   lengthwise
>   3 tablespoons butter *or* margarine
>   Chicken broth
>   ½ cup light cream
>   2 tablespoons all-purpose flour
>   2 tablespoons Dijon-style mustard
>   Hot cooked long grain and
>   wild rice

In skillet cook chicken in butter till tender, about 20 minutes. Remove to platter; keep warm. Measure pan juices; add enough chicken broth to make 1 cup. Return to skillet. Blend together cream and flour; add to broth. Cook and stir till thickened and bubbly. Stir in mustard. Spoon some sauce over chicken; pass remainder. Serve with rice. Garnish with tomato wedges and parsley, if desired. Makes 4 servings.

Microwave: In 12x7½x2-inch glass baking dish melt butter in countertop microwave oven 30 to 40 seconds. Add chicken; coat with butter. Micro-cook, covered, till tender, about 12 minutes; turn and rearrange chicken every 4 minutes. Remove to platter; keep warm. Measure pan juices; add broth to make 1 cup. Return to dish. Blend cream and flour; add to broth. Micro-cook, uncovered, 1 minute; stir. Cook till thick and bubbly, 3 to 4 minutes; stir every 30 seconds. Stir in mustard. Serve as above.

Baked Chicken Puffs

Cook ½ cup chopped **onion** in 3 tablespoons **butter.** Add 1 cup sliced fresh **mushrooms;** cook 2 minutes. Blend in 3 tablespoons all-purpose **flour,** ¼ teaspoon **salt,** and ⅛ teaspoon dried **rosemary,** crushed. Add 1¾ cups **milk.** Cook and stir till bubbly. Add 2 cups chopped cooked **chicken** or **turkey,** ¾ cup shredded **Swiss cheese,** and ¼ cup dry **sherry.** Heat and stir till cheese melts. Turn into four *ungreased* 1½-cup baking dishes. Beat 4 **egg whites** with ¼ teaspoon **cream of tartar** till stiff peaks form. Beat 4 **egg yolks** till thick and lemon-colored; add ¼ cup shredded **Swiss cheese.** Stir small amount of whites into yolks; fold into remaining whites. Pile atop chicken mixture. Bake at 375°, 15 minutes. Serves 4.

Turkey Soufflé

>   3 tablespoons butter *or* margarine
>   3 tablespoons all-purpose flour
>   1 teaspoon salt
>   ¼ teaspoon paprika
>   Dash pepper
>   1 cup milk
>   1 cup finely chopped cooked
>   turkey *or* chicken
>   1 tablespoon snipped parsley
>   1 teaspoon grated onion
>   3 egg yolks
>   3 stiffly beaten egg whites
>   2 tablespoons chopped onion
>   2 tablespoons butter *or* margarine
>   2 tablespoons all-purpose flour
>   ¼ teaspoon salt
>   ¼ teaspoon dried dillweed,
>   crushed
>   Dash pepper
>   1 2-ounce can chopped mushrooms,
>   drained
>   1¼ cups milk

Melt the 3 tablespoons butter in a saucepan. Blend in the 3 tablespoons flour, 1 teaspoon salt, paprika, and dash pepper. Add the 1 cup milk all at once. Cook quickly, stirring constantly, till thickened and bubbly. Remove from heat. Stir in turkey or chicken, parsley, and grated onion. Beat egg yolks till thick and lemon-colored. *Slowly* add turkey mixture to egg yolks, stirring constantly. Cool slightly. Add gradually to egg whites, folding together thoroughly. Turn into *ungreased* 1-quart soufflé dish. Bake at 325° till knife inserted off-center comes out clean, about 50 minutes.

Meanwhile, in a saucepan cook chopped onion in the 2 tablespoons butter till tender. Blend in the 2 tablespoons flour, ¼ teaspoon salt, dillweed, and dash pepper. Stir in mushrooms; add the 1¼ cups milk all at once. Cook quickly, stirring constantly, till thickened and bubbly. Remove soufflé from oven; serve immediately with sauce. Makes 4 servings.

For an impressive and elegant luncheon dish, offer ›
this golden-crusted, puffy soufflé. Light and rich in flavor, *Turkey Soufflé* is accented with a delicate dillweed and mushroom cream sauce.

Poultry For a Crowd

Cranberry Turkey Roast

An easy way to cook turkey for a crowd—

>   1 3-pound frozen boneless turkey
>   roast
>   • • •
>   1 16-ounce can whole cranberry
>   sauce
>   ¼ cup Burgundy
>   2 tablespoons brown sugar
>   1 tablespoon prepared mustard

Roast the frozen turkey roast according to package directions. Meanwhile, in a saucepan combine whole cranberry sauce, Burgundy, brown sugar, and mustard. Simmer, uncovered, for 5 minutes. Remove from heat.

To serve the turkey warm: Spoon *half* of the cranberry-wine sauce over turkey roast during the last 20 minutes of roasting time. Continue roasting till turkey is done. Place cooked roast on a serving platter; let stand 10 minutes before carving. Pass remaining sauce with warm turkey slices.

To serve the turkey cold: Roast turkey till done without spooning cranberry-wine sauce over during cooking. Remove cooked turkey from roasting pan. Refrigerate meat, uncovered, to cool quickly. When chilled, cover the meat. Chill cranberry-wine sauce. When ready to serve, slice chilled turkey and arrange slices on serving platter. Serve chilled sauce over turkey. Makes 10 to 12 servings.

Crockery Cooker: Thaw frozen turkey roast. Place turkey in an electric slow crockery cooker. Cover and cook on low-heat setting for 8 hours. Just before serving, prepare the sauce. In saucepan combine cranberry sauce, Burgundy, brown sugar, and mustard. Simmer, uncovered, for 5 minutes.

To serve the turkey warm: Remove cooked turkey to serving platter; let stand 10 minutes before carving. Spoon some of the hot sauce over turkey; pass remaining sauce.

To serve the turkey cold: Remove cooked turkey from cooker. Refrigerate meat, uncovered, to cool quickly. When chilled, cover meat. Chill sauce. Serve as above.

Chicken Drumstick Buffet

>   ⅓ cup butter *or* margarine, melted
>   2 teaspoons salt
>   24 chicken drumsticks (5 pounds)
>   1 12-ounce bottle chili sauce
>   (1½ cups)
>   1 cup water
>   ¼ cup finely chopped onion
>   2 tablespoons lemon juice
>   2 tablespoons Worcestershire
>   sauce
>   2 teaspoons sugar
>   ⅛ teaspoon cayenne

Combine melted butter and salt; brush drumsticks with butter mixture. Place chicken drumsticks in two large shallow baking pans. Bake at 375° for 35 minutes. Meanwhile, in a saucepan combine chili sauce, water, onion, lemon juice, Worcestershire, sugar, and cayenne. Bring mixture to boiling, stirring occasionally. Remove from heat. Spoon about ⅔ of the sauce mixture over drumsticks. Continue baking till chicken is tender, 15 to 20 minutes more. Reheat remaining sauce; spoon atop drumsticks. Makes 12 servings.

Barbecued Chicken Quarters

>   6 2½- to 3-pound broiler-fryer
>   chickens, quartered
>   Cooking oil
>   2 cups catsup
>   ½ cup finely chopped onion
>   ½ cup butter *or* margarine, melted
>   ½ cup molasses
>   ¼ cup vinegar

Brush chicken quarters with cooking oil. Season with salt and pepper. Place chicken, bone side down, on grill. Grill over *slow* coals for 20 to 30 minutes. Turn chicken quarters; grill until done, 20 to 30 minutes longer, turning occasionally. During the last 15 minutes of grilling, brush chicken occasionally with a mixture of catsup, onion, melted butter or margarine, molasses, and vinegar. Makes 24 servings.

Turkey Supreme

1 cup finely chopped onion
½ cup butter *or* margarine
1 cup all-purpose flour
1 48-ounce can chicken broth
　(6 cups)
2 cups light cream (1 pint)
1 teaspoon salt
⅛ teaspoon white pepper
4 beaten egg yolks
5 cups cubed cooked turkey *or*
　chicken
2 4½-ounce jars sliced mushrooms,
　drained
¼ cup chopped pimiento
　Toasted English muffin halves *or*
　toast points

In Dutch oven or 5-quart kettle cook onion in butter till tender but not brown. Blend in flour; stir in chicken broth, cream, salt, and white pepper. Cook, stirring constantly, till thickened and bubbly, about 15 minutes. Stir about *3 cups* of the hot mixture into egg yolks; return to hot mixture along with turkey, mushrooms, and pimiento. Cook and stir over low heat till heated through, about 5 minutes. Serve over muffins. Makes 16 servings.

Turkey Luncheon Squares

Cook a boneless turkey roast when you need cooked meat for casseroles, salads, and other dishes—

In a saucepan cook 1 large **onion,** chopped (1 cup), covered, in 1 cup **water** till tender, 8 to 10 minutes. Stir in 1 tablespoon instant **chicken bouillon granules** till dissolved. Set aside. In a large mixing bowl or kettle beat 12 **eggs;** add 3 cups **milk.** Blend in 4 cups soft **bread crumbs** (5 slices).

Stir in the onion-bouillon mixture, 8 cups chopped cooked **turkey** *or* **chicken,** 4 cups **cooked rice,** 4 cups **water,** 1 cup chopped **green pepper,** ½ cup chopped **pimiento,** 1 tablespoon **salt,** and ½ teaspoon **pepper.** Turn into two ungreased 13x9x2-inch baking pans. Bake at 325° about 1¼ hours. Cut into squares. In saucepan combine three 10¾-ounce cans condensed **cream of mushroom soup** and 1 cup **milk;** heat through. Pass sauce with turkey squares. Makes 24 servings.

Potluck Turkey and Rice Bake

Prepare one 2-pound frozen boneless **turkey roast** according to package directions and slice into 12 slices, *or* use 12 slices cooked **turkey.** Cook 8 slices **bacon** till crisp. Drain; reserve ¼ cup drippings. Crumble bacon; set aside. Cook 1 cup chopped **onion** in drippings till tender. Combine bacon; onion; 3 cups **cooked rice;** two 10-ounce packages frozen chopped **spinach,** cooked and drained; ½ cup sliced **celery;** and ¼ cup chopped **pimiento.**

Combine two 10¾-ounce cans condensed **cream of mushroom soup** and 1 cup dairy **sour cream.** Stir *half* into rice mixture. Turn rice mixture into 13x9x2-inch baking dish; arrange turkey atop. Spoon remaining soup mixture over. Top with mixture of 1½ cups soft **bread crumbs** and 2 tablespoons melted **butter.** Bake at 350° for 35 to 40 minutes. Serves 12.

Crowd-Size Chicken Fried Rice

4 cups long grain rice
1 5-ounce bottle soy sauce (⅔ cup)
¼ cup cooking oil
½ teaspoon salt
3 cups finely chopped cooked
　chicken *or* turkey
¾ cup finely chopped green onions
　with tops (1½ bunches)
1 4-ounce can chopped mushrooms,
　drained
6 beaten eggs
2 tablespoons cooking oil

In Dutch oven combine rice, soy, the ¼ cup oil, salt, and 7 cups water. Bring to boiling; stir once or twice. Cover tightly; reduce heat and simmer till rice is tender and liquid is absorbed, about 14 minutes. Remove from heat. Divide rice mixture between 2 large saucepans. Combine chicken, onions, and mushrooms; stir *half* into each pan. In a 12-inch skillet cook eggs and ¼ teaspoon salt in the 2 tablespoons oil till well cooked throughout, lifting and breaking up eggs with spatula. Remove from heat. Using a pastry blender, break up eggs into tiny pieces. Stir *half* the eggs into each pan of rice mixture. Cook over low heat, stirring occasionally, till heated through. Makes 16 servings.

Poultry Postscripts

Create appetizing soups, sandwiches, salads, and casseroles using leftover cooked chicken and turkey. Just be sure to store the meat properly to maintain its good flavor.

Wrap meat loosely or place in a covered dish, then refrigerate promptly. Or, wrap meat tightly in moisture-vaporproof material, such as heavy foil or freezer bags; seal, label, and freeze. If the bird is stuffed, remember to remove stuffing and meat from the bones as soon as possible. Store meat, stuffing, and gravy separately. (See storing and thawing tip, page 51.)

INDEX

A-B